This is number one hundred and ninety-eight in the
second numbered series of the Miegunyah Volumes
made possible by the Miegunyah Fund
established by bequests under the wills of
Sir Russell and Lady Grimwade.

'Miegunyah' was Russell Grimwade's home from 1911 to 1955
and Mab Grimwade's home from 1911 to 1973.

Frances Burke

DESIGNER OF MODERN TEXTILES

Nanette Carter and
Robyn Oswald-Jacobs

THE
MIEGUNYAH
PRESS

THE MIEGUNYAH PRESS
An imprint of Melbourne University Publishing Limited
Level 1, 715 Swanston Street, Carlton, Victoria 3053, Australia
mup-contact@unimelb.edu.au
www.mup.com.au

First published 2021
Text © Nanette Carter and Robyn Oswald-Jacobs, 2021
Images © various owners, various dates
Design and typography © Melbourne University Publishing Limited, 2021

Designed by Daniel New
Printed in China by 1010 Printing Asia Pty Ltd

A catalogue record for this book is available from the National Library of Australia

9780522877113 (hardback)
9780522877120 (ebook)

Contents

Frances Burke fabrics

for the

SMALL HOME
MODERN FAST COLOURS
OBTAINABLE at

NEW DESIGN PTY. LTD.
46 Hardware Street, C.1.
Tel. MU 1872

also
FURNITURE
POTTERY
LAMPS

This advertisement appeared in a 1953 booklet, *Costs and Quantities of a Modern Home,* published by the Small Homes Service of the RVIA and *The Age.* Run by architect and critic Robin Boyd from 1947, the service offered affordable house plans and architectural services.

Foreword

In the pantheon of twentieth-century Australian design, Frances Burke stands tall. She was a major force—a brilliant designer, a technical innovator for her craft, a champion for progressive textile design not just for the home but also for settings devoted to health, hospitality and community, and a supremely successful retailer and business owner. Internationally, she deserves to be better known. Her work can be placed alongside celebrated mid-century designers of printed fabrics like Austrian émigré Josef Frank, who worked for Svenskt Tenn in Sweden, Alexander Girard for Herman Miller in the USA, and Vuokko Nurmesniemi and Maija Isola for Marimekko in Finland.

Why? Not just because she designed and sold her fabrics under her own name for more than thirty years but also because, as Nanette Carter and Robyn Oswald-Jacobs show us in this beautiful book, Frances Burke was a pioneer in the interpretation of Australian indigenous themes in modern textile design. While her experiments with such themes can be compared to Sydney-based fabric designers Alexandra (Nan) McKenzie and Anne Outlaw of Annan Fabrics, who from 1941 also explored native flora and fauna and Aboriginal motifs, Burke's Aboriginal-influenced designs like *Snake and Dugong* (1938–39) and *Rangga* (1940), amongst many others, preceded and outlasted the production of their Sydney counterparts. Burke's practice also predated Gerard Herbst's work with Prestige from 1946 and Claudio Alcorso's promotion from 1947 of his firm's 'Modernage' fabrics range of Australian-influenced designs by thirty-three artists, including Margaret Preston, Russell Drysdale and James Gleeson. In short, Frances Burke was a pacesetter: she made textile design her life—from 1937, first with Maurice Holloway, then from 1942 under her own name until she retired and closed her business in 1970.

The role of textiles, especially curtains, in histories of the modern interior is often underplayed. Furniture and lighting designers feature heavily, as does the work of architects and interior designers who deploy bespoke fittings and fixtures or signature colours and surfaces. The textured backdrop of fabrics (invariably rendered feminine), like their positive acoustic properties, go relatively unheard. Joel Sanders has even written in *Harvard Design Magazine* 'curtain wars',[1] where designers and historians of the modern domestic interior have glossed over practices 'sustained by profound social anxieties about gender and sexuality'. In the Australian setting then, this book thus fills an important lacuna. But there is also a special caveat to a discussion of Burke's work with respect to the modernist canon: it is her fascination with and her reluctance to entirely give up figuration. Unlike the abstractions of Bauhaus weavers Gunta Stölzl and Anni Albers, and locally the eclarté textile company founded in Melbourne in 1940, whose preoccupations were subtle gradations of colour in the warp and weft of weaving, Burke's facility and forte was colour and two-dimensional representation in printing. As Carter and Oswald-Jacobs quote, for Burke, colour was 'a living joyous thing—it vibrates', and she applied this passion across three decades. Flowers and leaves, the Pacific islands, marine, nautical, aeronautical and indigenous motifs, as well as abstract designs and even *Black Opal* (1965) all formed part of Burke's comprehensive suite of sources from the 1930s to the late 1960s. And it was this painterly quality and loyalty to the figurative that was her strength, the clue to her commercial success, and also, arguably, her critical limit.

Frances Burke gives a vivid account of Melbourne's design culture from the 1930s to the 1950s, the pivotal role played by instructors such as Napier Waller and Michael O'Connell at Melbourne Technical College (now RMIT University), the city's various art schools, the National Gallery School and the George Bell School, both of which Burke attended, and the significant role played by shops and department stores such as Georges, Myer and Hicks Atkinson. Part of Frances Burke's success was her readiness to immerse herself in her city's design and architectural culture. In 1947, influential friend and patron Maie Casey opened Burke's stylish shop 'New Design' at 55 Hardware Lane in central Melbourne. Remarkably, the arch and two flanking doorways with their box-like alcoves above, one for 'Showroom', the other 'Office', still exist, perhaps the only remaining physical evidence of her presence in the city today.

Burke's fabrics appeared not just in architect-designed houses but also in public and community buildings, from hospitals and theatres to company towns and ski lodges. Their ubiquity points to the respect with which scores of architects and their clients, locals and émigrés alike, showed for Burke's designs. Her fabrics entered the living rooms of countless everyday suburban Australians. They also entered mine. The living room of my parents' 1959 CHI Home in Beaumaris, with its Stegbar Windowall, Caneite ceiling and open fireplace with its exposed copper flue designed by my father and made locally in Mordialloc, had Frances Burke curtains as its feature backdrop. My parents bought the grey–green *Shields* pattern fabric at the Myer Emporium. They made a good choice. The same fabric appeared in émigré architect Ernest Fooks's office in Woonsocket Court, St Kilda and at journalist Eve Gye's home, also in Beaumaris. Burke's designs had national reach: their appeal was professional and popular.

Some of Burke's designs, even during her lifetime, became classics in their own right. Many of these should still be in production. Patterns like *Crossways* and *Squares* seem utterly contemporary. *Tiger Stripe*, for one, still appears as lively and vital as it was when first released in 1938. For too long, the achievements and contribution of Frances Burke have been hidden from view. Her partnership with Fabie Chamberlin, her social, artistic and professional milieu in Melbourne and the context of textile design across postwar Australia, and her prodigious design output have never been fully documented. Now, unearthed from the archives and systematically presented in this book through Carter and Oswald-Jacobs' empathetic and meticulous research, Burke's brilliant career has been brought back to life.

Philip Goad
Professor and Chair of Architecture
Redmond Barry Distinguished Professor, University of Melbourne

The Goad family in their living room, 1962.

1

FINDING HER WAY

A portrait of the young, determined Frances Burke.

esigner and businesswoman Frances Burke was a dynamic, feisty person; articulate, with a resonant, commanding voice, distinctive enunciation and a unique way of expressing herself. Her bright blue eyes focused directly on those around her. Diminutive in height, with her light blond hair invariably styled in a French roll, she was always elegantly dressed and was excessively fond of hats. Burke had a zest for life and loved her chosen career; she was good company and a loyal friend. Anne Purves, director of the respected Melbourne art gallery Australian Galleries and a friend of Burke's, described her as 'extreme but something of a legend. She didn't suffer fools gladly but she mellowed.'[1] Another friend, historian Marjorie Tipping, remembered her as a fascinating character who nevertheless could be difficult. 'Not a lot was readily disclosed … she kept a lot to herself.'[2] Confident in the expression of her sexuality, Burke was wryly described by author and bookseller Philip Jones as 'chic and almost out'.[3] A complex person with a strong drive to succeed, Burke was a catalyst for change and loved engaging with new ideas and cultivating new friends. Generous with her support of younger designers, she enjoyed communicating her passionate interests in design and the arts.

An undated pen and ink sketch by Burke.

THE BURKE FAMILY

Born on 10 January 1904 in Spotswood, a suburb west of Melbourne, Frances Mary Burke was the youngest of three children. Her father, Francis Henry Burke, was a tailor's presser and her mother, Frances Veronica (Brown), was a former tailoress. Since three members of the family were named Frances or Francis, confusion may have been commonplace! Burke's sister Vera was six years older and her brother Charles four years. During her childhood the Burke family lived in Brunswick and Coburg, then largely working-class suburbs, north of Melbourne, where Frances attended local Catholic schools for both her primary and secondary education.

In later life Burke recalled that her father worked in sales at the women's clothing manufacturer and importer Burrell, Watkinson & Co. located at 118 Flinders Lane, the centre of the textile, clothing and fashion industries in Australia. With obvious pride, Burke recalled many years later that as a young girl she would walk to meet him on his return from work and accompany him home. The samples of fabrics that Burke's father brought home from work left an enduring impression on the young Frances. She explained that the rag trade 'caught my attention and interested me from a young age … something which I always thought I would be part of … the aura of Flinders Lane was around our lives'.[4] As interior decorator Margaret Lord, a contemporary of Burke, wrote in her memoir and design manifesto *A Decorator's World*, 'Certain visual experiences in early life have a lasting importance'.[5] Burke remembered that fabrics were regularly passed around the family to be 'felt, looked at and understood', often discussed as part of dinner-table conversation.[6] Her mother and sister Vera made their own clothes from fabrics Burke's father brought home which, with her mother's skills, enabled them to be 'dressed beautifully with a great deal of flair'.[7] Making no mention of her own dressmaking skills, Burke instead claimed to be an avid museum visitor from an early age, suggesting the beginnings of the inherent curiosity that characterised her adult personality.

Sydney Road, Coburg, seen from the corner of Bell Street in 1915. Growing up in the neighbourhood, Burke would have been familiar with this lengthy shopping strip.

Burke described her family life as 'well-ordered, well-thought out' but, more forebodingly, said her parents were 'rather enclosed, not encouraging closeness'.[8] Her characterisation of her father as 'a bit of a dandy, interested in the ladies', might appear to be a throwaway line, except for a 1918 court report detailing a case that her mother brought against her husband for maintenance for herself and fourteen-year-old Frances. The case disclosed, according to the *Brunswick Leader,* 'a most unhappy state of affairs during the whole of the 20 years of the married life of the partners'.[9] Payment of one pound per week for her mother and ten shillings per week for Frances were ordered along with court costs, plus a £25 surety against dereliction of payment, implying a history of financial neglect by Burke's father. Growing up in the financial uncertainty of a single-parent household, at a time when women's wages were far less than men's, coupled with her father's lack of support, despite her evident admiration for him, explain Burke's determination to be self-reliant as an adult.

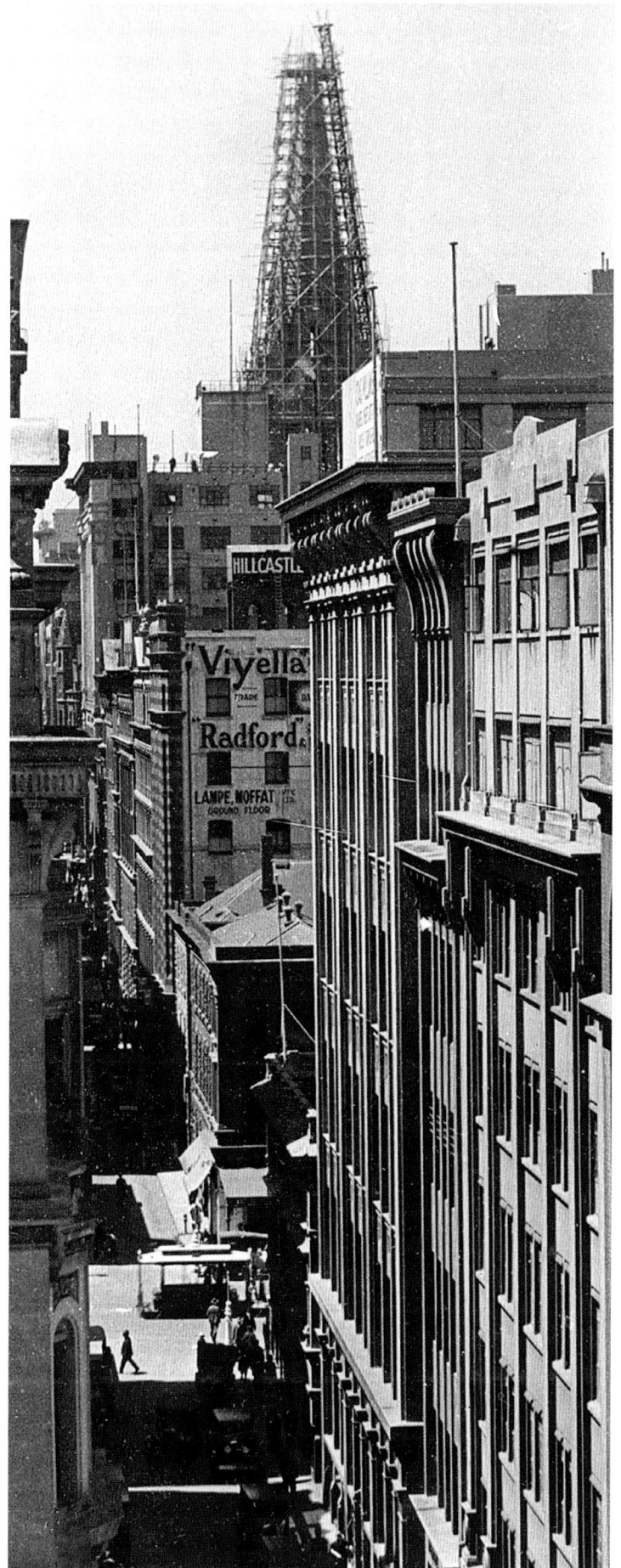

Flinders Lane with St Paul's Cathedral spire under construction in 1931. The narrow street was the busy centre of Melbourne's rag trade, fabric supply and garment-making for most of the twentieth century.

STARTING OUT: MEETING FABIE

It is likely that Burke's independent spirit led her to begin a career in nursing, rather than embarking on training in the textile or clothing industries, as might have been expected from her early connection with that world. She could have made this choice for a number of reasons but most likely for the financial security it offered. It is thought she began her training at the Mount St Evin's Private Hospital (now St Vincent's Private) in Victoria Parade, Fitzroy, and then moved to the widely recognised, well-regarded 100-bed Homeopathic Hospital at 250 St Kilda Road, Melbourne, where she qualified as a registered nurse in April 1927. She later claimed to have nursed Dame Nellie Melba at Mount St Evin's, but more importantly it was there she formed a close friendship with fellow nurse Frances Mary (Fabie) Chamberlin.

Chamberlin had grown up in the regional city of Geelong in a lower-middle-class family; her father was described as a 'general agent' and her uncles were also engaged in business. Chamberlin's father had served in World War I and been gassed at Villers-Bretonneux. Shortly after his return in 1919, Chamberlin's mother died after a long illness, and eleven-year-old Fabie became a boarder at the Sacred Heart School at the Convent of Mercy in the inner suburb of Newtown. Although she was a diligent student, Chamberlin's passion was for music and she aspired to a career as a concert pianist. At some point the decision was made that instead she would begin training as a nurse.

Chamberlin explained that their families were already friends before she and Burke began nursing:

A hand-coloured photographic postcard of the purpose-built Melbourne Homeopathic Hospital where Burke completed her nursing training in 1927.

We met through Frances's mother, a wonderful person,
a friend of my aunt … She encouraged us to take a
flat in Jolimont. I'd come from Geelong. We were
different but we had a lot in common. We had mutual
friends and separate ones. We could always rely on
one another, there was no truer, more loyal friend than
Frances to me or me to her.[10]

According to close friend Diane Masters (Romberg), Burke and
Chamberlin offered one another 'untiring praise and undying
moral support'.[11] Together they created a loving home where
daily domestic arrangements were smoothly organised and
where comfort was assured.

After sharing their first flat in 1930, the pair moved a number
of times within the neighbouring inner suburbs of Jolimont
and East Melbourne. They remained together for sixty-seven
years, until Burke's death in 1994. Burke and Chamberlin were
accepted as a gay couple by their social circle but neither spoke
openly on the record about their sexuality. Anne Purves recalled
that 'Frances and Fabie were strong enough to carry it off … not
being victims … mostly it was handled fairly discreetly, they
were very natural about it … It was talked about that they were
lesbians, it wasn't commonplace.'[12] During the early twentieth
century there

An undated pencil drawing of Fabie Chamberlin signed by Burke.

was no specific backlash against lesbians … Rather,
there is a pervasive historical 'silence' about any actual
or possible lesbian presence in society, perhaps helped
by the lack of criminal sanctions to lesbianism and a
belief that if it was ignored, it would go away. In artistic
and upper-class circles, female relationships were
discreetly pursued and largely ignored by others.[13]

Unlike so many women artists of that period, Burke did
not pay a high price for her creative freedom. Disappointment,
loneliness and financial precariousness are not necessarily
conducive to a full and vital creative life, and it is clear that Burke
benefitted from the support, in her life and work, of the loyal
Chamberlin who was homemaker, helpmate and, later, business
partner. In the early years of the twentieth century, women
were expected to marry rather than pursue a career: 'The social
conditioning of women prepared them for traditional marriage
and motherhood and any formal education they received was
regarded as being a good influence on the next generation.
Those women who had successful careers either remained single
or had atypical marriages.'[14] Burke and Chamberlin together
created a satisfying alternative to traditional marriage, and
Burke's education, rather than having an influence on offspring,
supported her creative and professional life.

AN INHERITANCE: ART AND DESIGN EDUCATION

In 1932 Burke's mother died, leaving her three children a shared inheritance of £1265 12s 4d, which, along with the reflections on mortality that the loss of a parent brings, provided the impetus for a change of direction in Burke's life the following year. Four hundred pounds was just above the average annual wage of that year, not a huge sum but enough to provide the three siblings with a degree of financial security. While she continued nursing, this timely inheritance allowed Burke to immerse herself in a multifaceted creative life, giving her a sound basis for the career she would later choose in textile design and production.

Gallery School students including Burke's friends Phyl Waterhouse and Alannah Coleman, painting in the still-life classroom of the Gallery School, 1935.

THE GALLERY SCHOOL, 1933

By 1933 Burke was taking drawing classes at the Gallery School, located in a humble single-storey structure beside the impressive, extensive building that housed the National Gallery of Victoria, the State Library of Victoria and the Melbourne Museum. The director, Bernard Hall, had been guiding the Gallery School since 1892 and had maintained the school's teaching of academic traditions, resisting aspects of modern art that might lead to abstraction. Experimentation was discouraged; accepted genres were portraiture, landscape, still life, biblical stories, oriental scenes, historical themes and sedate scenes of contemporary life.

Gallery School students came from many backgrounds and were attracted by the relatively low fees, ease of enrolment and casual hours. They were required to successfully complete the drawing course, which meant copying from plaster casts of antique statuary before moving onto painting. It appears that, like many others, Burke didn't move beyond the drawing course but she was proud of her training; it meant, in her own words, that she was 'very well-equipped on the technical side ... able to draw very well'.[15]

According to art historian Janine Burke, despite its shortcomings the Gallery School, taught artists what they needed to know, which was:

> to reject what is inessential to your vision, to capitalize on your talents and to discard or disguise your failings ... learn how to consciously change the culture for the better ... how to transform what you have learned into a vivid, living, individual statement that will nourish and intrigue you for the rest of your life.[16]

Burke painting at an easel using a palette and rest stick in the early 1930s.

Melbourne Technical College students in the 1930s, including Janet (Bardin) Robinson, seventh from the left in the front row, who became a lifelong friend to Burke after meeting her in class.

The purpose-built School of Applied Art at the MTC opened in 1916.

Burke's portrait of William Splatt, a fellow MTC student and trainee architect who later became a noted educator.

MELBOURNE TECHNICAL COLLEGE, 1933–36

In 1993 Burke also began part-time study in the School of Applied Art at Melbourne Technical College (MTC), conveniently located opposite the Gallery School in La Trobe Street, learning lino-block and silk-screen printing. Her work was considered exemplary, and she was awarded the college's art scholarship in November 1934, which was renewed in the two following years. In later life Burke recalled: 'I originally trained to be a fine artist and I had a very, very thorough training. I went to RMIT then called the Melbourne Technical College. It did, have a very strong art and design section. Some very, very good and powerful teachers were there.'[17]

The strength of the school in those years was due to a commitment by the head Harold Brown to attract established artists to teach there. Two particularly important artist-craftsmen instructors Burke encountered were Napier Waller and Michael O'Connell. Waller was a leading mural painter and designer of the widely admired *I'll Put a Girdle Round About the Earth* mosaic mural (1933) commissioned by Sir Keith Murdoch for the façade of Newspaper House at 247 Collins Street, Melbourne. Waller had pioneered lino-block printing in Australia and Burke printed her first fabric lengths using this technique. O'Connell was known as a watercolour artist and for hand-crafted garden ornaments and furniture made of coloured concrete. In the early 1930s he became a fashionable designer and fabric printer, using large lino blocks to print heavy Irish linen, often producing his own fabrics in the studios at MTC. While it is not certain that Burke took his class, she must have seen his work and known other students who studied with him.

Burke clearly benefitted from her time at the Gallery School and MTC by developing lifelong friendships with other students. At the Gallery School she met Joan Lindsay, who later became famous as the author of *Picnic at Hanging Rock*, and even more importantly Maie Casey, who was married to conservative politician Richard Casey and already a significant patron of modern Australian art and design. Burke and Maie Casey became lovers, remaining such close friends that they rang one another daily at 9.15 a.m. Melbourne time, wherever Casey was in the world, for the rest of their lives. Through the highly sociable and energetic Casey, Burke would have met furniture designer Fred Ward and others engaged in designing furnishings and modern interiors, including artist Sam Atyeo and perhaps socialite and gallery manager Cynthia Reed. In 1936 Burke and Casey both left the Gallery School and began studying at the private George Bell School.

Acknowledging George Bell's positive influence, Burke recalled that he 'showed me what creative art was'.[18]

GEORGE BELL SCHOOL, 1936–38

George Bell was a graduate of the Gallery School, and he subsequently spent sixteen years studying and successfully exhibiting in London and Paris before returning to Melbourne in 1920. During the economically difficult years of the Depression, Bell and fellow artist and critic Arnold Shore opened an art school in an upstairs studio in Bourke Street near Queen Street, which soon became a magnet for aspiring artists. This collaboration ceased in 1936 with Bell opening a school from his home in Selborne Road, Toorak.

Respected for his acceptance of new ideas, technical knowledge and 'astringent integrity',[19] Bell was known as a teacher who encouraged his students' individual development. He provided a nourishing environment both socially and creatively for the more than one thousand talented and diverse artists who studied with him in the course of his career.[20] In addition to meeting older artists Will Dyson and Mary Cecil Allen at Bell's classes, Burke met contemporaries including Eric Thake, Eveline Syme and Guelda Pyke, and made friends with Russell Drysdale, Maisie Newbold, Alan Sumner, Yvonne Atkinson, Bob Pulleine and Peter Purves Smith.

Bell's teaching helped liberate Burke from the constraints of her early training at the Gallery School, encouraging her to pursue a more individual approach. She explained that 'his great power was this, that he liberated your mind. He didn't make you a copy of himself nor expect you to be. In fact he hated that. He taught you to think and act for yourself and be creative which is a very, very important thing later.'[21]

At his invitation-only Thursday Club, Bell discussed modern art theory, in particular the need for a strong emphasis on form and the exploration of new approaches to colour and line. Burke explained Bell's influence on her approach to art:

> I was all the time with my head in a book and it was George who taught me to think of the actual result and to create from my own mind and thoughts … at the Thursday classes he would set a theme and you would have to create a picture from it.[22]

Casey wrote that 'Most of all he made his students brave; released them from timorous inhibitions.'[23] Bell was known to refer to Burke affectionately as 'Little Burke', a play on both her stature and the name of a busy thoroughfare in the Melbourne city grid, Little Bourke Street.

Painting en plein air: Burke seated with an unidentified man and woman, likely at an art camp.

Ford was a major client of the Catts Patterson advertising agency, where Burke worked 1936–37. The auto manufacturer targeted women as potential owners from 1925 when its cars were first produced in Australia.

Bacchante (c. 1933), a single colour lino-block print by Michael O'Connell featuring a series of 'units' filled with decorative motifs.

ADVERTISING EXPERIENCE

While attending the George Bell School in 1936, Burke gave up nursing and took a job as an office manager with Catts-Patterson, the Melbourne branch of a successful Sydney advertising agency. Her responsibilities involved managing the workflow of the agency—handing out jobs, checking their completion and organising the transfer of finished artwork to bromides for the printers. Advertising executive Betty Blunden, who was just starting her successful career as an art director, recalled that 'Burke was an organiser, she did not art direct us … She did not have any creative input at all'. It was with some astonishment that Blunden later discovered Burke had a creative talent when she started her textile design and printing business.[24]

In retrospect, Burke's choice to work in advertising was prescient, since at that stage she had not made any specific decisions about textile design or business. As advertising historian Jackie Dickenson explained: after working in advertising creative women 'could utilise design, illustration and copywriting skills picked up in the industry for cultural production'.[25] In Burke's case it appears that working in advertising helped her develop what is now understood as a personal brand. This included the naming of her business; linking her designs with her identity by using her crisp cursive signature on the selvedge of her fabrics; and positioning herself as an expert on design for the modern home through media interviews and writing. Blunden commented that in 1936 Burke was 'older and more worldly, but not the least bit smart … There was an extraordinary change of personality when she became creative', explaining that 'she looked smashing' once she had launched her business.[26] Chamberlin recalled on the other hand that 'Frances always dressed well' and that she had her clothes made at Melbourne's elegant Georges department store in fashionable Collins Street.[27]

AN OPPORTUNITY

Burke was inspired to embark on a career in designing and producing textiles, later recalling 'its appeal is universal. It will be art that can get right in among the people.'[28] It wasn't a rash change of career, but a carefully reasoned decision based on her awareness of a gap in the Melbourne market. British artist and craftsman Michael O'Connell had already established a successful business producing high-quality textiles printed with original designs. But when he and his Australian wife Ella left for England in early 1937 to attend celebrations in honour of the coronation of George VI in May of that year, an opportunity arose. As architectural historian Harriet Edquist wrote, 'With her astute business and excellent design skills Burke rapidly filled the vacuum created by O'Connell's departure.'[29] It was even more fortunate for Burke that the O'Connells decided not to return.

Flowers, leaves and fronds

Inspiration from a wide range of garden flowers, leaves and fronds formed the basis of many of Burke's earliest designs. *Bouquet* (1937), one of her more conventional designs, combined bunches of the cottage garden flowers with diagonally crossed trails of ivy—an approach deriving from decorative traditions going back to the Renaissance. Others employed a more abstracted style, such as *Palm* (1943), with its graphic sawtooth fronds contrasted against the negative space of the background. Ferns, sunflowers, lilies and magnolias were plants Burke used a number of times, carefully observing and playfully exploring their forms to develop varied designs.

Burke frequently contrasted motifs of solid colour with the motif in outline, as in *Dahlia* (1940). Another technique she employed was to represent a bloom in stages—half open and in full flower—as seen in *Sunflower* (1937), or even in six stages, as in *Belladonna* (1940). A design called *Canna Leaf* (1940) took another approach—tracing highlights and shadows over the contours of the plant, resulting in a lively interplay of lines. It appeared in a range of versions and colourways over decades, suggesting that designs based on this common garden plant not only reflected Burke's enthusiasm but that it was also commercially successful. Sometimes Burke chose to use two colours for *Canna Leaf*, printing the form of the leaves in one colour and the outline in a contrasting colour.

Exotic and tropical plants like *Palm, Poinsettia* (1937) and *Hibiscus* (1940) appeared in Burke's early work, since her fabrics were often purchased in bulk by fashion retailers Georges department store and the Myer Emporium to be made up into summer and resort wear. Wearing these flowers that bloomed in the tropical north of Australia and the Pacific Islands suggested luxurious holidays that became increasingly unlikely with the outbreak of World War II in 1939. In the postwar period Burke used mostly Australian native plants, responding to popular nationalist sentiment, but she also developed a series of designs based on the rose and the oak leaf, which retained strong associations with England.

Australian native flora appearing in designs such as *Banksia* (1939) and *Waratah* (1940) exhibited a range of styles. The early *Gum Blossom* (1937) had a homely Arts and Crafts style, using naturalistic colours of green and red. *Waratah* combined alternating rows of single flowers enclosed by a leaf either side into a discrete oval shape, with the waratah's curling petals suggesting Art Nouveau, a style popular in the early twentieth century in Australia. Initially it was used as a large motif in a cyclamen colour on unbleached linen furnishing fabric in 1940 for a Myer Emporium furniture promotion. In 1955 Burke printed *Waratah* again, on a far smaller scale, in black over a shot fabric producing an updated, dramatic effect.

Dahlia (1940)

Canna Leaf (1940)

Bouquet (1937)

Sunflower (1937)

Belladonna (1940)

Palm (1943)

Waratah (1955)

2

FORGING
A CAREER
IN DESIGN

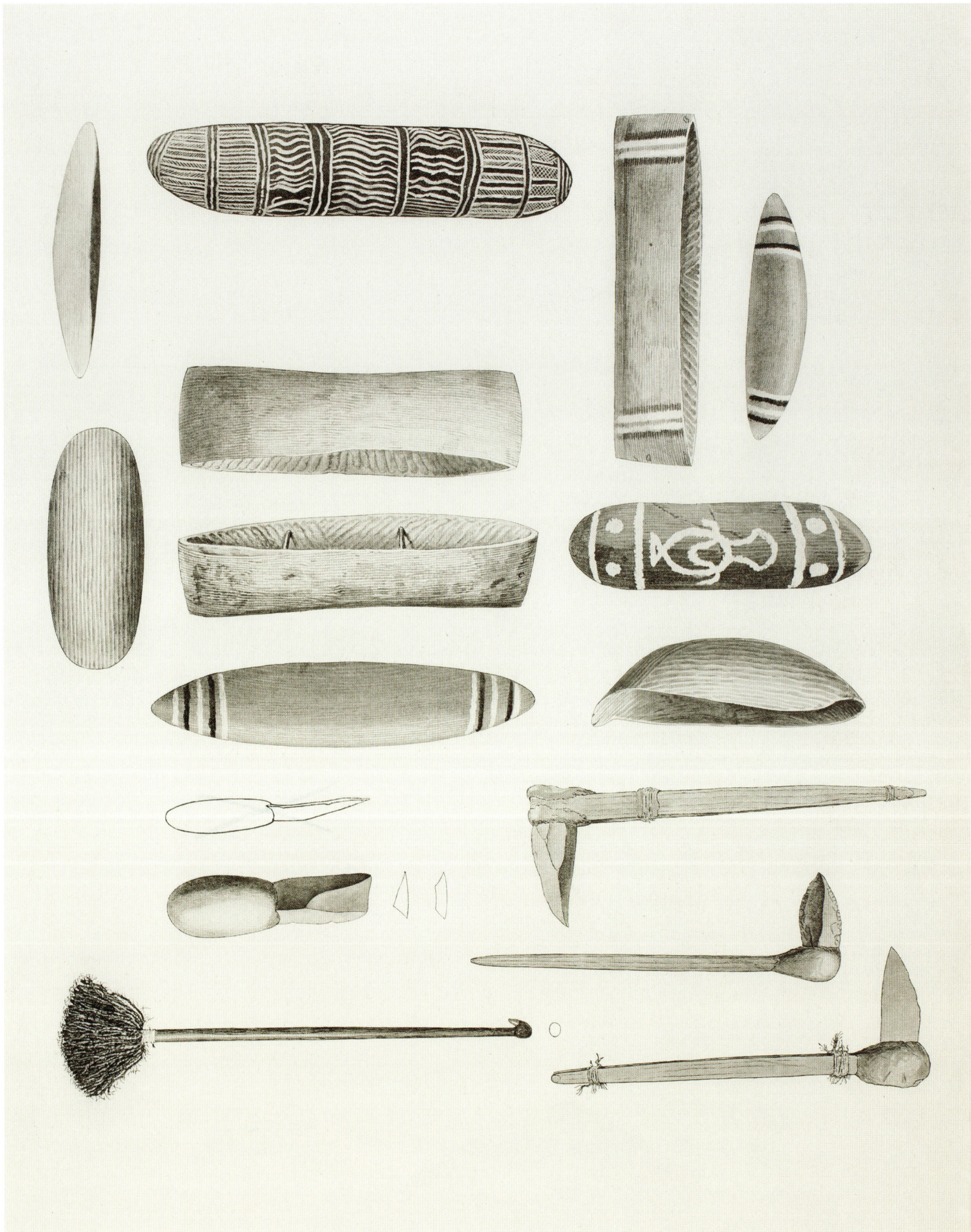

ike many young artists and designers of the 1930s, Frances Burke took advantage of the three major cultural institutions in the city of Melbourne: the State Library, the National Gallery of Victoria and the National Museum of Victoria. Together they occupied a city block between Swanston and Russell streets, adjacent to the Melbourne Technical College (MTC). At the museum she began sketching objects in the ethnographic collections for inspiration in producing decorative designs. It is likely that with her growing interest, Burke would have visited the occasional exhibitions of Indigenous culture appearing in small private galleries around Melbourne throughout the 1930s. She later claimed to have read the work of pioneering anthropologist W Baldwin Spencer.

These drawings of objects collected by W Baldwin Spencer and Frances James Gillen were prepared for their 1904 book *The Northern Tribes of Central Australia*. The majority of the collection of Indigenous culture on display in the Melbourne Museum, that Burke drew from in the 1930s, was supplied by Spencer.

The building housing the State Library, the Melbourne Museum and the National Gallery of Victoria photographed from the corner of La Trobe and Swanston streets during the late 1930s.

Georges façade showing the three entrances of the U-shaped arcade with its elegant displays of fashionable merchandise, leading to the entrance where a doorman would greet and guide prospective customers to the department of their choice.

PIERRE FORNARI: EXPERT ENCOURAGEMENT

Burke often explained that it was comments made by the charming Pierre Fornari, fashion designer and fashion coordinator for Georges department store, reported in a 1937 *Herald* article that inspired her to make an appointment with him. Fornari had been quoted as saying that Indigenous Australian artefacts at that time on show at a Paris exhibition of commercial art might influence fashions, suggesting that elegant women might wear clothing 'reproducing the soft colours and unique designs of bull-roarers, spears, native armlets and basketry, and embroidered versions of clay designs with which the aboriginal adorns his limbs and chest for corroboree'.[1] At the meeting, Burke showed Fornari her sketchbook of designs based on Aboriginal and Pacific Island exhibits in the Melbourne Museum. According to Burke in a 1980 lecture, Fornari used her fabrics for unique 'glamour garments', which appeared in Georges' extensive display windows.

In a 1940 interview Burke explained that she had sent fabric featuring her handpainted designs to be exhibited in Paris, possibly at the 1937 Exposition Internationale des Arts et Techniques dans la Vie Moderne.[2] She had also shown them around Melbourne and, as a result, had received her first order for printed fabrics. Since this first order was from Georges, it seems likely Burke showed both her sketchbooks and textiles to Fornari.

More significant was a fortuitous conversation Burke had shortly afterwards with a saleswoman at Georges, a Miss Lawson, who sought her assistance: 'Fornari is only using your designs for a luxury fashion novelty, which mightn't last. Why don't you come down to earth and design some materials for our sportswear department?'[3] Lawson requested that Burke produce designs in commercial quantities, pleading: 'we desperately want materials because we're short of them … Won't you try and do something for us?'[4] The shortage of fashionable imported textiles was due to a punitive trade tariff established by the Commonwealth Government to reduce imports and shore up the nation's trade deficit during the Depression, which lingered in Australia into the late 1930s. Burke considered the request, and later recalled:

Well I could draw and I could design and I knew in a way, how to put a block onto cloth and make it look like a printed thing and so I sailed in and got a length of cloth which was an absolute disaster! It couldn't have been worse … As I was working on sixty yards of their material I had to run around … and buy sixty yards of material that looked like it and go to someone and say 'What went wrong?'[5]

That someone was a textile chemist, employed at either Yarra Falls Mills in Johnston Street, Abbotsford, or Leeds Dyeing and Chemical Works in Westgarth Street, Northcote, who gave her detailed professional advice on dye chemistry and showed Burke and future business partner Maurice Holloway how to do it the right way.

Fashion coordinator for Georges department store Pierre Fornari and his golf partner Miss Cairnes at a society event at the Sorrento Golf Course in 1934.

DECIDING ON DESIGN

At the same time as developing a folio of designs and drawings, Burke was considering options for her future—making the decision in favour of textile design in 1937. An undated set of reflections, titled 'Two Year Plan for Living', in Burke's handwriting at the back of a sketchbook appears to have been written in a single session prior to Burke establishing her business, but perhaps after the first orders were delivered to Georges.[6] The writing is a powerful stream-of-consciousness account; an honest sorting of facts and feelings in the decision-making process of a young woman at a crossroads in her life. It shows a depth of self-awareness, strength of purpose and insight. Since she noted that it 'all depends on securing a congenial job', it is likely to have been written early in the year, before she went on to register her business in July 1937.

The 'Two Year Plan for Living' starts as an exploration. As her thinking quickly evolved Burke listed her assets and her liabilities, including 'attitude to design' and 'knowledge of fashion demands' along with 'material design', 'apparel arts' and 'industrial arts'. Evidently the decision to become a textile designer was made at this point, as she went on to consider colour and the choice of motif: 'nature', 'geometrical', 'floral', 'tropical'. The alternatives of two- or three-dimensional pattern were weighed up. Burke's capacity to envisage textiles as three-dimensional objects, hanging in folds but also in relation to the proportions of a space and other elements within, is suggested—an emerging ability that became fundamental to her practice. By the end of her soul-searching process she had clearly committed to design.

The independent Burke, who needed to support herself despite the small inheritance from her mother, was clearly pragmatic with considerable physical and mental energy, intelligence and a robust self-confidence that enabled her to sum up her emerging parallel abilities as those of a businesswoman and designer rather than an artist and craftswoman. This was the basis for the position she created for herself as a 'bridge' between modern design and industry that would underpin and drive her career, and make her a figure of national significance.

On the basis that design would be her life's work, Burke finished her 'Two Year Plan for Living' with a plea:

TO Whom it may concern

Give me what I'm asking for

Clear Head Clear Vision

Clear discrimination that I shall not waste my time on inessentials

Peace happiness security Stability in purpose—progression from year to year

Burke sized up her talents and abilities as marketable items and considered her needs, her passions and particularly her independence. She made both a personal and a calculated business decision when deciding to become a textile designer.

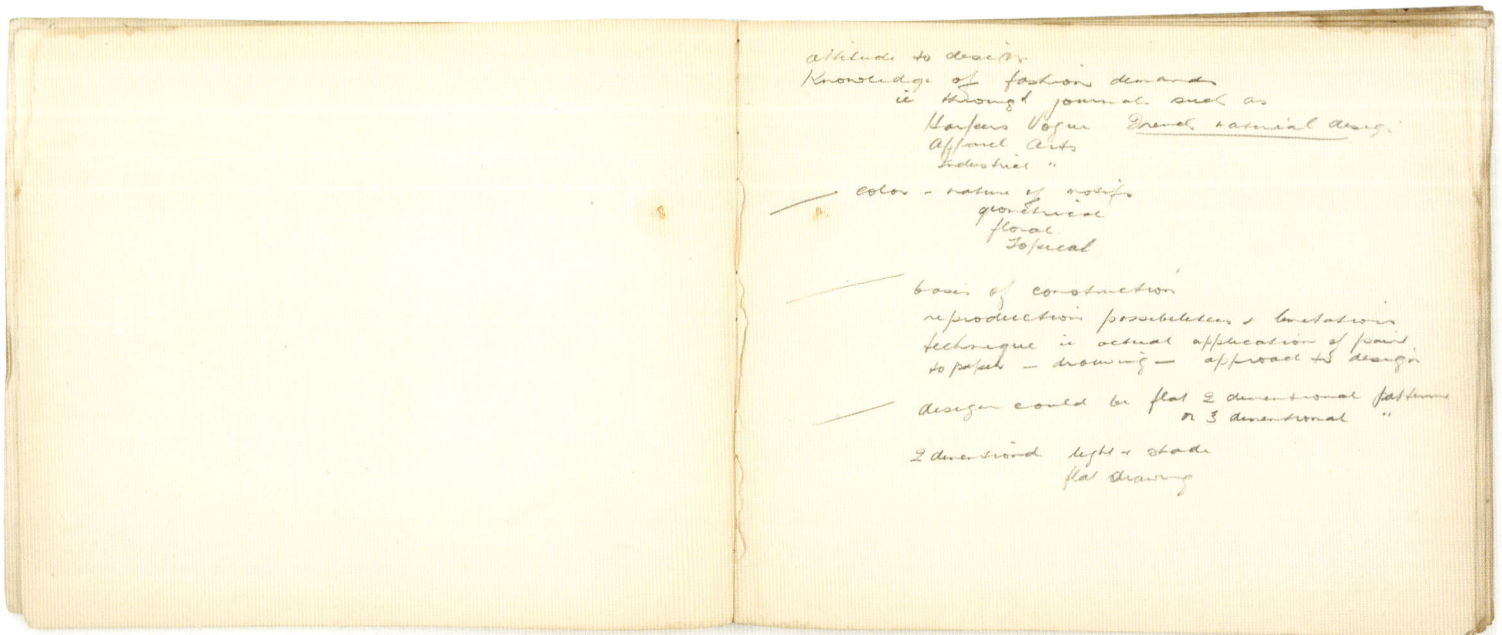

Burke's 'Two Year Plan for Living' was found at the back of a partly used sketchbook when her effects were accessioned by the former Textile Resource Centre at RMIT University.

2 year Plan for living

The situation therefore is this

① The urgency of getting a congenial job
an attitude of mind that will make for
security, hope + ambition

② An objective

③ unhampered living conditions in
pleasant surroundings

④ a collection of friends likely to be
part of this development

⑤ substantial interest + affection

all depends on securing congenial job
ability to hold it — sincerity in
developing it

assets for application are
necessity — genuine ability to design
average intelligence in learning
executive capacity

liabilities — nerves - reaction to
fellows - bad memory - readiness to
down tools   lack of genuine objective
+ enthusiasm

BUSINESS NAMES ACT 1928.

Business Name ___BURWAY PRINTS___ BURWAY TEXTILE PRINTS   Registration No. **67899**

Nature of Business ___Hand printed fabrics___

Address ___55 Hardware St. MELB.___   125 COLLINS ST, MELBOURNE.
___Stalbridge Chambers, 443 Lit. Collins St. Melbourne.___

Date of Filing.	Document and Details.		No. of Doc.
5.8.37	A. 4.8.37	FRANCES BURKE and	
		MAURICE BASIL HOLLOWAY	1.
6.4.42	G. 6.4.42	MAURICE BASIL HOLLOWAY retired	2.
24.4.42	G.June 1940	Add. changed to 434 Little Bourke St.	
		Melbourne	3.
23.9.42	G. 23.9.42	JANE HOWELL WILLIAMS became a member	4.
5.6.44	G. 5.6.44	FRANCES MARY CHAMBERLIN became a member	5.
26/9/51	G. 1/10/51	C/business name as above	6.
8/11/51	G. /1/51	C/add as above	7
26/7/56.	G. 24/2/56.	CHANGE OF ADD. AS ABOVE.	8.

J .234/4.35.—4580.—5M.

The business registration card for Burway Prints showing a new name
and changes of company members and addresses.

A silk screen showing layers of previously printed designs, including
'Greetings from Burway', which was probably printed on paper or card.

SETTING UP IN BUSINESS

Burke established a business in partnership with Maurice Holloway, a fellow MTC graduate, which was registered on 5 August 1937 as Burway Prints; the nature of the business was recorded as 'Hand printed fabrics'. It appears that Holloway became responsible for printing, with Burke focusing on the designs and colours, and the marketing, publicity and financial aspects of the business. The partnership was described in a 1940 article: 'Miss Burke designs and [Maurice] concerns himself with blocks and printing; a good working partnership, for neither transgresses into the field of the other.'[7]

While the first commercial order of 60 yards of printed fabric for Georges was a technical failure, it was a salutary lesson for the resourceful Burke and Holloway. It led directly to the development of their method for printing and processing light and wash-fast fabrics with available dyes. A newspaper article reported Burke's first commercial production of textiles, suggesting a 'breath of Cannes and the Lido will be brought to Melbourne's fashionable beach resorts this season'. The article presented the efforts of Burke and Holloway in developing an effective printing process in a way that introduced some mystery and left out Holloway's contribution:

> After months of experimenting in her attractive studio home—a loft over the stables behind one of East Melbourne's substantial old homes—Miss Frances Burke, a young Melbourne artist of the modern school of painting has [begun] … with the idea that dyeing was similar to painting. Miss Burke soon discovered that the application of dyes to linen was a hard task compared with paint to canvas … the application of suitable fast dyes, fast to light and water, has meant months of patient experimenting … After she has completed a design, it is transferred to a block, from which it is finally printed onto the material. Before these materials are marketed they are laundered by a special method, which includes boiling. Behind the success of these novel and fashionable creations is the secret of the printing process, which, naturally she will not reveal.[8]

The importance of employing light-fast dyes was Burke's focus in this initial stage of her business. It was widely known that the dyes used by Michael O'Connell were 'fugitive', subject to rapid fading. According to Yvonne Atkinson, one of Burke's friends from the George Bell School, O'Connell's fabrics were available at a Manchester Lane shop:

> we were always having to re-dress [the] little window because O'Connell's dyes did not stand up to the sun —a pity, because his designs and colours were rich and beautiful. Frances Burke was destined to take over his

market … she had no problem with her dyes; she very rightly never compromised with artistic license. The colours were always gay and fresh. Her hard work and tenacity reaped their reward.[9]

After initially working from the home Burke shared with Chamberlin, she and Holloway set up a print studio on the sixth floor of Stalbridge Chambers, 443 Little Collins Street in late 1937, remaining there for three years. While it seems unusual for a fabric-printing studio to be located in legal chambers, Price & Chamberlin barristers and solicitors were a major tenant of the building, suggesting that Burke received an entrée through Chamberlin's family. Conveniently, the building had a lift, was only a block from a cluster of businesses attracting affluent women, including the Primrose Pottery Shop and the Wattle Tearooms, and was not far from the Myer Emporium that had in 1939, like Georges, begun to commission Burway fabrics to make into fashionable beachwear.

Burway Prints was established on the sixth floor of Stalbridge Chambers in Melbourne's legal precinct, but was close to fashionable small shops, galleries and cafes.

Snake Totem (c. 1940), a design showing the influence of Northern Australian Aboriginal bark paintings in the motif of the snake, the dotted marks and symbols representing waterholes or meeting places in the Indigenous source.

Burke and Holloway would test the design, stencil and colours on paper before printing on fabric, as in this paper proof for *Dugong and Boomerang* (1940–41).

Unusually for Burke, *Bouquet* (c. 1937–40) used four colours.

The interior of Burway Prints early in the 1940s, with a range of Burke's fabrics, from florals and nursery prints to Indigenous-inspired designs, in the foreground.

Burke displaying a range of her striking fabric designs in the early 1940s.

PRINTING TECHNIQUES AND FABRICS

Burke and Holloway adopted O'Connell's use of lino blocks to print the heavy Irish linen that they preferred as a ground fabric. On a previous trip to London in 1929 O'Connell would have seen the handprinted fabrics produced by a number of small studios, including Footprints and Crysede. Block printing was an economic alternative for smaller studios, avoiding the commitment of 10-yard runs needed to make machine printing viable. The use of block printing ensured that the craft tradition continued to play an active role in bespoke and small volume printed fabric production in England.

Lino-block printing requires a design to be drawn then cut and carved into a piece of linoleum, which is then flocked and usually glued to a block of wood for stability during printing and for durability in handling.[10] The areas cut away become negative spaces in the design; dye is applied to the raised areas of block, which is then laid firmly on the fabric—sometimes with the help of a mallet—so that the design is transferred to the fabric. The registration of the blocks—the way in which they fit together to create the design in repeat—is achieved using a pin or a nail attached to the block, which is then aligned by the printer.

World War II was announced two years after Burke made her decision to pursue a career in printed textile design and establish a business, then prove that there was a market for her fabrics. The scarcity created by bans on imported printed fabrics during the war strengthened her business. Author and historian Peter Cuffley wrote that during the war years 'Melbourne's Frances Burke had been building a reputation for the design of handprinted fabrics, and by the early 1940s was widely known'.[11] In fact, as Burke later stated with some chutzpah, 'there can be nothing on earth more satisfactory for a business person than to have a monopoly!'[12]

The shortage of fabrics and dyestuffs during the war years was challenging for designers and printers. Egyptian and Japanese cottons became unavailable, so did linen from Egypt and Ireland. However, the Indian Ocean was still open to shipping so it was possible for Burke and Holloway to import Indian cotton, a fabric similar in weight to a light calico, and other printing supplies. In an interview later in life, Burke recalled how she and her staff were confronted with evidence of the battles raging across the world when they would receive bags of glue from the Middle East with shrapnel in them.[13]

The purchase of fabric by the yard was a difficult proposition for shoppers, given wartime rationing, as the National Council of Clothes Styling determined the amount, quality and dimensions of fabric and pattern pieces allowed for men and women. To save purchasers' valuable rationing coupons, Burke sold hemmed fabric pieces, ostensibly furnishing fabric, which by unpicking the hems could easily be converted to whatever garment customers chose. The lack of up-to-date goods in mainstream stores meant

Georges Gazette from November 1937 showing the earliest commercial use of Burke's designs—in resort wear for the Australian summer.

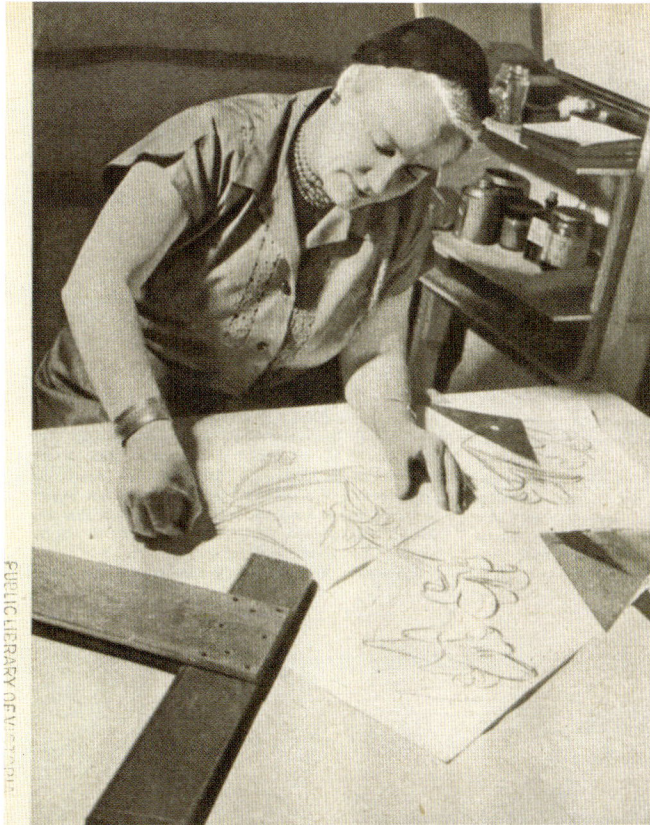

It's easy for a trained artist with the talent of Frances Burke to work out designs for fabrics. She uses pencil, oil paint or, as is shown here, a crayon. This design is called lilium auratum.

This Frances Burke design is called "Crete." It was based on a Cretan jar and colors are Stone-age Grey, Tribal Brown with a banana palm motif, and Chartreuse with a distinctive white spot design.

Her colors are for Australians

BY ESME JOHNSTON

"COLOR is the ideal way to express this bright, sunny land of Australia."

That's what Frances Burke told me as she leaned on the desk of her small Melbourne textile factory.

Frances Burke, ex-artist who studied at the Victorian National Gallery and with painter George Bell, turned to fabric design because she felt oils didn't give her enough range of contact. Today her "Burway Prints" are pioneering a new (for Australia) type of decor, gay, colorful and as Australian as the birds, the shells, the aboriginal motifs which she designs and prints on her materials.

"American women have cheerful and well-designed domestic interiors and better domestic gadgets which give a lift to their morale and allow them more time to call their own," says Frances Burke. "I want that kind of thing for Australian women who, in general, have to take what they can get — and like it."

She feels that her neat little factory with its scientific equipment and its Heath Robinson stove, known affectionately as "Mrs. Murphy," is a step in the right direction. It is, at least, devoted to industrial design, the new profession which in America, she says, is as clearly defined as medicine or the law. If she can't yet produce labor-saving appliances, she can bring color into the homes of her countrywomen.

Much research into the dye question has been done by Miss Burke and her production manager, Miss Jane Williams. The result is a color range (and there is nothing newer in America today) which is fast to sun, light, washing. Dyes are weighed to .005 of a gram, and they are constantly working out new nuances of shade and toning. They work for a new color
— *(To page 12)*

LEFT: Here are some new Frances Burke colors. Blue-violet with horizontal stripes, Hot Pink, Orchid (the little green native variety), and Sea-grey Blue. These colors can be used alone or in combination.

Feb. 13, 1950—WOMAN'S DAY— Page 11

Burke drawing lilies in preparation for a design in 1950.

Gordon Shebly stoking the stove, affectionately named 'Mrs Murphy',
to help dry the fabrics as Margaret Lawrence hangs them out.

an engaging shopping experience at Burke's studio. As wartime shortages worsened, cotton became more acceptable as a 'go anywhere' fabric—in addition to Burke's popular cotton beach and playwear, Georges even carried ball gowns in cotton.

In December 1941 Japan's bombing of Pearl Harbour led to the outbreak of the war in the Pacific. Australia's introduction of compulsory military service in the following year meant Holloway was called up and, perhaps fearing the worst, he withdrew from the business. When Holloway returned from his brief period of enlistment as a part-time member of the Home Guard, rather than rejoin Burke, he chose to make his own way in business. He established a printing firm called Veronica Textiles in 1947, renaming it Textile Converters in 1956 when he went into partnership with textile designer Bee Taplin. They produced work for a range of clients, including Burke. Holloway also developed a selection of his own Indigenous-influenced designs that appeared in a 1948 exhibition at Australia House in London. They also appeared in a 1952 exhibition at the Rockefeller Center in New York curated and designed by Australian expatriate Dahl Collings. Along with work by Burke and Sydney textile and screen-printing business Annan Fabrics, the exhibition featured Indigenous Australian implements, bark paintings and photographs of Australian Aboriginal people of Central and Northern Australia. Following this exhibition, however, apart from a complex cubist wall-hanging based on a Picasso painting produced in 1960,[14] Holloway focused on printing the designs of others for the remainder of his working life.

Meanwhile, Burke restructured the business, listing Jane Williams as a partner in 1942 and adding Chamberlin as a third partner in 1944. After joining Burway Prints in 1938, Williams had been trained by Holloway to prepare the dyes and print the fabrics; her duties also included organising a group of talented staff including Janet (Bardin) Robinson, Margaret Lawrence, Dorothea Vowells, Dorothea Allnutt and Gordon Shebly. A frequent travelling companion and friend to Burke, Williams was crucial to the business, and she continued in partnership with Burke and Chamberlin for the remaining twenty-seven years of its operation.

Margaret Lawrence preparing the stencil on a silk screen.

By the early 1940s Burke's fabrics were mostly screen printed rather than block printed. Screen printing had been developed in the United Kingdom in 1907 as a process to print longer runs easily and less expensively than could be managed by block printing.

At the Burway studio the screen-printing process was undertaken completely by hand. A wooden frame was made slightly larger than the motif or the repeat being printed, to which silk or organdie was accurately stretched and secured. The design was applied using a stencil or was transferred onto the screen using a light-sensitive film or emulsion. A sealed area around the edge of the motif provided a well for the dye to be passed across with a squeegee, which needed to be the full width of the motif. Depending on the weight of the fabric, and therefore the rate of absorption, between one and four passes of the squeegee was needed. Screen printing was an affordable process, allowing flexibility for 'the creative and imaginative designer … putting on cloth extremely varied ideas and effects … there is virtually nothing that can be painted on paper that cannot be screen printed on cloth'.[15]

A separate screen was needed for each colour; for the design to 'read' properly the screens needed to register together. On one side of the print table, to which the fabric was attached, was a metal guide rail with clamps, which were set for correct registration. Since screens were comparatively cheap to make and colours easily changed, designers could present a range of colourways giving the commercial client or individual customer the luxury of choice.

Gordon Shebly and Jane Williams pulling a squeegee across the screen for *Oak Leaf Stripe* (1950).

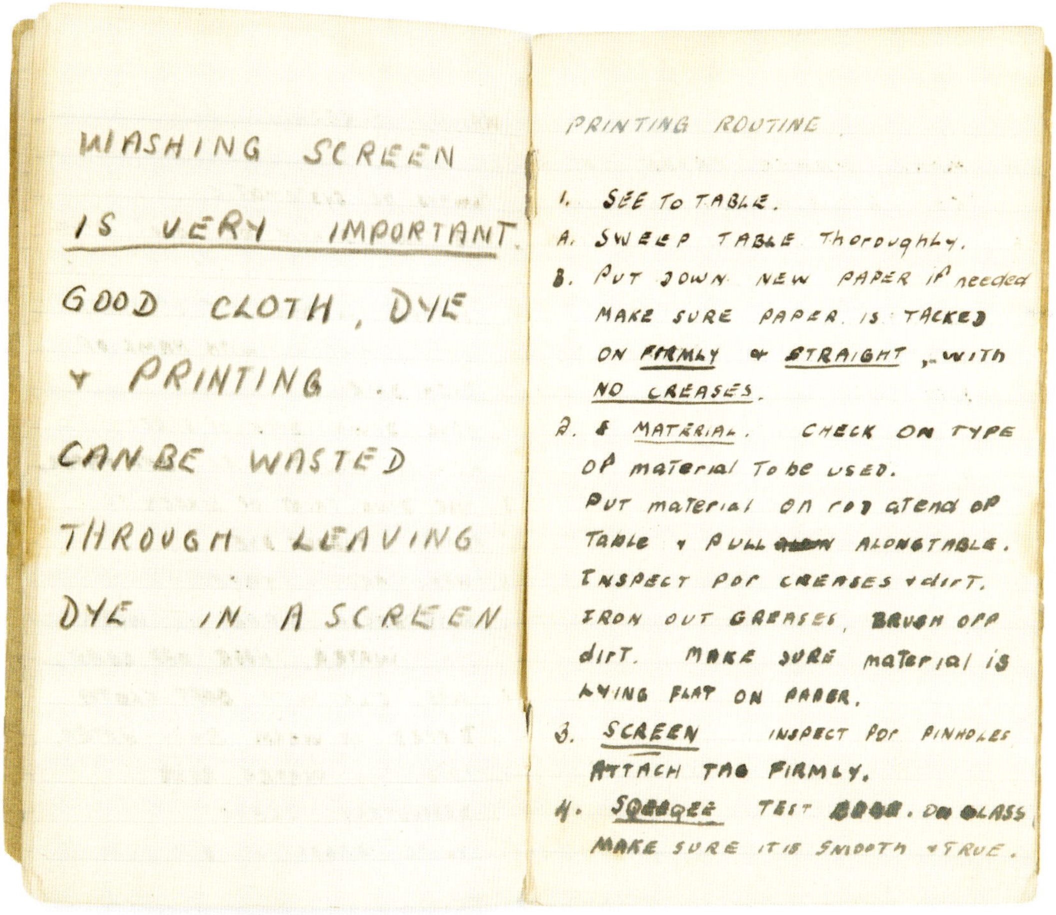

WASHING SCREEN

IS VERY IMPORTANT.

GOOD CLOTH, DYE

& PRINTING

CAN BE WASTED

THROUGH LEAVING

DYE IN A SCREEN

PRINTING ROUTINE

1. SEE TO TABLE.
   A. SWEEP TABLE Thoroughly.
   B. PUT DOWN NEW PAPER if needed
   MAKE SURE PAPER IS TACKED
   ON FIRMLY & STRAIGHT, WITH
   NO CREASES.

2. & MATERIAL. CHECK ON TYPE
   OF material To be USED.
   PUT material ON rod at end OF
   TABLE & PULL ALONG TABLE.
   INSPECT FOR CREASES & dirt.
   IRON OUT CREASES. BRUSH OFF
   dirt. MAKE SURE material is
   LYING FLAT ON PAPER.

3. SCREEN INSPECT FOR PINHOLES
   ATTACH TAG FIRMLY.

4. SQUEEGEE TEST EDGE ON GLASS
   MAKE SURE IT IS SMOOTH & TRUE.

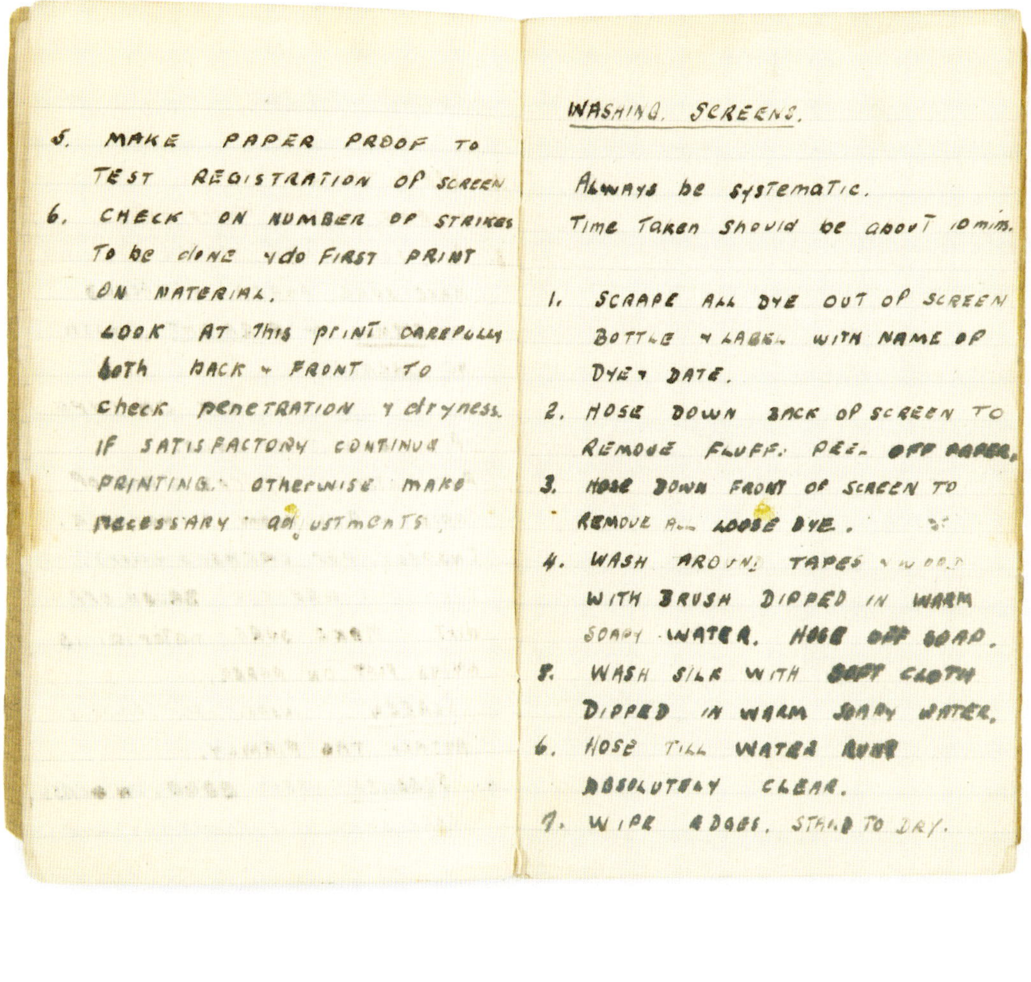

---

5. MAKE PAPER PROOF TO
   TEST REGISTRATION OF SCREEN
6. CHECK ON NUMBER OF STRIKES
   To be done & do FIRST PRINT
   ON MATERIAL.
   LOOK AT THIS PRINT CAREFULLY
   BOTH BACK & FRONT TO
   check penetration & dryness.
   IF SATISFACTORY CONTINUE
   PRINTING. OTHERWISE MAKE
   NECESSARY adjustments.

WASHING SCREENS.

Always be systematic.
Time Taken should be about 10 mins.

1. SCRAPE ALL DYE OUT OF SCREEN
   BOTTLE & LABEL WITH NAME OF
   DYE & DATE.
2. HOSE DOWN BACK OF SCREEN TO
   REMOVE FLUFF. PEEL OFF PAPER.
3. HOSE DOWN FRONT OF SCREEN TO
   REMOVE ALL LOOSE DYE.
4. WASH AROUND TAPES & WOOD
   WITH BRUSH DIPPED IN WARM
   SOAPY WATER. HOSE OFF SOAP.
5. WASH SILK WITH SOFT CLOTH
   DIPPED IN WARM SOAPY WATER.
6. HOSE TILL WATER RUNS
   ABSOLUTELY CLEAR.
7. WIPE EDGES. STAND TO DRY.

Pages from Gordon Shebly's notebook
detailing the procedures he was required to
follow at Burway in 1949.

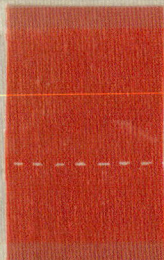    

PANHANDLE RED   BRICK   RED-CLIFF   PINK BLOOM   WAXFLOWER

CENTRE RED - 8co   ROCK RED   BURNT ORANGE   HOT PINK   CENTRE RED   CARNATION

MOLE   POTATO   TOBACCO   PINK STONE   TRIBAL BROWN   PRUNUS

OCHRE   BANKSIA   WET SAND   PUTTY   LEAF GREY   COOTAMUNDRA

BAZIL BROWN   YARRA GREEN   LICHEN GREEN   COPPER GREEN   DARK LEMON   LEMON YELLOW

CLEAR AND BOLD: COLOURS AND DYES

Colour to Burke was 'a living joyous thing—it vibrates'.[16] With her art training and the influence of George Bell's teaching in particular, she was confident in her selection of colour and hue. Anne Purves observed that 'Frances Burke's designs were like her: clear and bold. They were primary coloured, the colours were strong but not extraordinary; you couldn't separate the colours and the designs. They were innovative, modern and suited to simple materials; they were much in demand.'[17]

Burke continued to work closely with the dye chemist she and Holloway had consulted early on to develop her chosen colours, weighing and measuring the ingredients of the dyestuff and carefully recording the results to ensure light-fast and wash-fast results.

> I was good at maths, which permitted me to do the formulas to work out the mathematical processes [of using dyes] … I had some sort of inbuilt capacity so that I could switch over from the rather dreamtime of painting into the cold practicality of production. Then I learned about business. Maurice and I were just his [the dye chemist's] 'cup of tea'—to be his guinea pigs … he taught me about dyestuffs. There is an enormous change between paint and watercolour and a chemical thing like a dyestuff.[18]

Burke's range included a colour called Bad Black, which was a slightly off-black, named because it had proved impossible in the 1940s to obtain the concentrated black that Burke preferred. With marketing acuity, Burke capitalised and the distinctively named Bad Black became an extremely popular colour. Burke's fabrics became known for their colours: 'Compared with … the patterns coming out from England these new beach fabrics were bold and bright. They caught on.'[19]

Colour charts of Burke's 36-inch colour range showing the colours from which clients might choose designs to be printed (c. 1958).

The Myer Emporium became Melbourne's largest department store when
the new eight-storey building opened in 1933.

EARLY DESIGNS AND SUCCESS

Rather than the Indigenous Australian and Pacific–inspired designs that Burke had originally shown Pierre Fornari, the themes Georges initially chose to commission were more conventional, though they were modern in style. An article in *The Herald* reported that Burke had 'given special thought to Australian tastes and conditions'. These included marine themes of a seahorse, a starfish and wave, dolphins and mermaids 'captured in nets'. Flower prints included the poinsettia, 'a brilliant scarlet flower making an all-over pattern on a white ground … used for play suits, beach jackets and even swimming suits'. There were also designs based on jungle scenes of tigers, one of monkeys in a tropical scene of coconut palms and beach, and another of 'Siamese dancing girls, dragons and pagodas … in a rich dark red colour'.[20] A 1940 Georges catalogue showed that the store later accepted the Indigenous Australian and Pacific themes, the kind she had shown Fornari in 1937.

By successfully addressing popular taste in her designs and colours, Burke's first textiles were a commercial success. She recalled receiving 'an enormous amount of publicity through Georges and through the various displays in Collins Street and then Myers came to me'.[21] The Myer Emporium, with branches in Bendigo and Adelaide, had a far bigger clientele than Georges, resulting in larger orders for fashion fabrics. Myer also began selling Burke's furnishing fabrics in its exclusive Rocke furniture section, where they could be selected by staff designers for interiors commissioned by affluent clients.

Burway Prints continued to prosper through the war years. Burke's increasing focus on furnishing textiles, modern designs in brilliant colours and strong, earthy tones defined an emerging Australian style. Loyal staff member and lifelong friend Janet (Bardin) Robinson explained:

> There was no material coming in during the wartime; her designs were so colourful, so crisp and clear cut, such a nice change from what was available … shadow tissue and the like. She was selling all she could produce, making a living and supporting a staff of five or six people. She was a very enthusiastic driving force.[22]

A press release for the 1952 exhibition of modern Australian fabrics at the Rockefeller Center in New York reported: 'Frances Burke admits that with her small staff she cannot supply the demands for her fabrics, but prefers to keep her work at the stage of production where she can give it the individuality and careful finish of the hand craftsman.'[23] Despite these comments on the quality of Burke's production being related to craft, the increased demand for her work in the postwar period saw her contracting out the printing for a period in the late 1940s and again in the early 1950s to allow her time to focus on design and writing, which was gaining her considerable publicity as an expert on design and the modern home.

Georges advertisement from *The Herald*, January 1939, showing Burke's use of marine themes for beach clothing and swimsuits.

A program for the Myer Emporium's Spring Carnival of Fashion of 1939 including 'cruise frocks' in Burke fabrics.

Advertisement in *The Home* magazine for Orient Line cruises to the Pacific, March 1937.

"There's a boy coming home on leave

"He'll enjoy coming home on leave" if you make it "ten days of heaven." Be sure to own a gay colourful creation that will be a striking foil to his weeks of blue or khaki. He will carry away a joyous picture of you in a happy setting of glowing floral design, if you wear any of the floral frocks from Georges Younger Set Salon, priced from 39/6 (left hand sketch typical) to 55/6. These are chock full of fashion interest—gathers, pockets, pleatings, bows, frills—or if that sounds too too femme for 1940, think in terms of tailored detail. If you can reconcile your purse and conscience to the work of developing Australian talent, decide on a Francis Burke print, handblocked in high style with Australian motifs, aboriginal or floral, at £5/19/6. (Right hand sketch is Bathurst Island Tribal motif.)

HULLO HOLLYWOOD! Call that Californian bluff, in a "Sandese" Picnic frock. "Sandese" you know is crush-proofed and does not need pressing. Each frock or play suit is conceived in three play colours, toned to a perfect contrast. Take the skittish young illustration—pink blouse, green sash, mauve skirt. Typical at 37/6.

A *Georges Gazette* edition of 1940 illustrating dresses in Burke fabrics. *Tapa Flower*, the design on the right, is described as a 'Bathurst Island tribal print'.

Pacific-influenced designs

Following the lead of British designer and artist Michael O'Connell, Burke was inspired by the patterns of Pacific tapa cloth in some early fabric designs. Dividing the space of a design into a grid of variously sized cells within which a range of decorative motifs were used and re-used in different combinations was an approach that suited the lino-block technique. Designs with clear borders in a single colour meant that repeats didn't need to be disguised and registration was made easy.

Burke's Pacific-influenced designs like *Samoa* (1938), *Tapa Flower* (1938) and *Tapa Cloth* (1938) were inspired by the ethnographic collections of the Melbourne Museum but were also symptomatic of a popular interest in the cultures and natural beauty of the Pacific Islands and New Guinea. In the early 1930s goldmining had commenced in Papua under the colonial administration and Australian investors were gaining huge dividends. The economic potential of Australia's near neighbours generated enthusiasm about the future of the region and its peoples. While a small number of affluent Australians had taken Pacific cruises when they were introduced in the 1920s, in the following decade when P&O and its subsidiary Orient Line began marketing them to middle-class Australians, cruises became extremely fashionable. Buoyed by its success in this market, Orient Line commissioned a new series of ships promoting travel as a modern leisure activity. The ships were fitted out by emerging designers including New Zealand architect Brian O'Rorke and American designers E McKnight Kauffer and Marion Dorn.

Throughout the 1930s, Pacific Island cultures were exploited for stories and music in Western popular culture and for imagery and patterns in fashionable goods. There was international fascination for the filming of *Mutiny on the Bounty* in Tahiti in 1935, starring Hollywood heart-throbs Clark Gable and Franchot Tone. Paris fashions incorporated touches of Pacific materials and motifs—correspondent Olga Drossinos reported in *The Home* in January 1936 that couturier Jacques Heim had designed an exciting series of accessories—'exotic bracelets and necklaces in carved sandalwood or shells, ropes of fine white shells worked into flowers, and sandals and headgear inspired by the South Sea Islands.'[24] In 1939 staff of the Myer Emporium were being encouraged to attend a film on Polynesia as a training event, while its staff magazine offered instructions on how to sell the new range of Pacific-influenced goods about to flood its stores. Burke's tropical-themed *Jungle* (1937–38), a design initially used for beachwear and later for tablecloths, may have featured in Myer's range.

Burke continued to explore using grids in her designs, even after moving on from references to Pacific Islands and taking up the silkscreen printing technique. *Bird and Tree* (1940), for example, was a design in which she alternated a highly stylised tree motif with a phoenix and left a number of cells bare. In this design the twisty lines that form the grid are as dominant as the motifs, an approach that Burke returned to in designs such as *Moresque* (1941), *Alpine* (1947) and *Snowflower* (1960).

Tapa Flower (1938)

Samoa (1938)

Bird and Tree (1940)

Jungle (1938)

Tiger Lily (1940)

3

DEVELOPING
A NATIONAL
MARKET

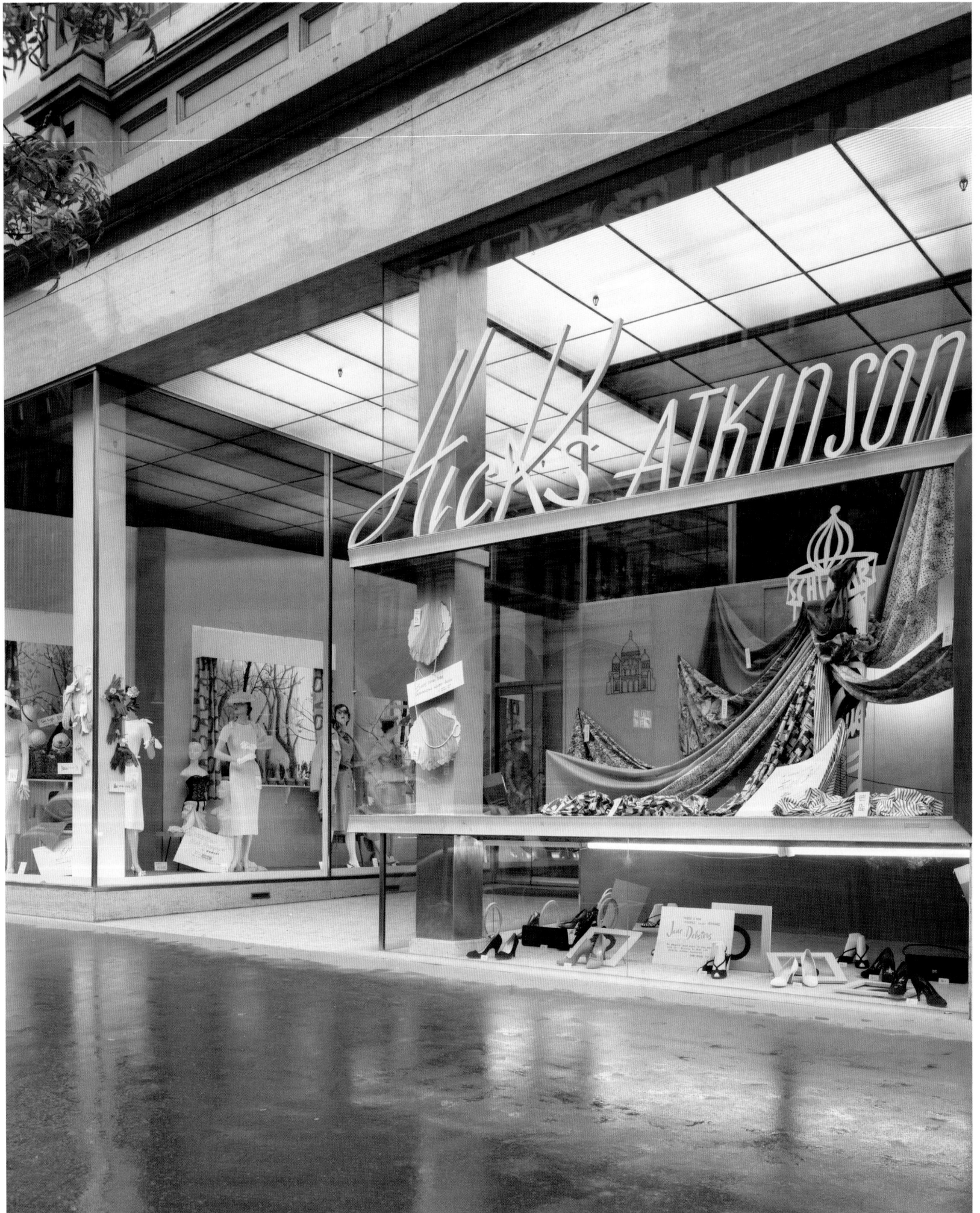

rances Burke began by wholesaling her fabrics, supplying a single department store, retailing through Victorian Arts and Crafts Society exhibitions, and selling to a small number of clients who found their way to her studio. Her capacity to supply high-quality fabrics with increasingly accomplished modern designs during World War II, when imported printed fabrics were unavailable, encouraged her to expand her market in Melbourne and beyond. When the war ended, despite the resumption of imports and a difficult economic climate, Burke continued developing the market for her fabrics around Australia, in towns, regional centres and the various state capitals. In the postwar period Burke was well placed to benefit from the impending boom in home building. Curtains, bedspreads and cushion covers, in designs and colours that fitted the mid-century modern style, were embraced by a generation of young homeowners, discerning designers and emerging architects.

The Hicks Atkinson department store located in Melbourne's Collins Street was known for its stylish merchandise and visual marketing until it closed in 1963.

Myer Emporium's furnishing fabric department displaying Burke's fabrics including, *Waterlily* and *Phoenix* (c. 1939–49).

Burke's *Rangga* featured in the 1941 exhibition 'Australian
Aboriginal Art and Its Application' at David Jones.

CITY DEPARTMENT STORES AND REGIONAL TRADERS

Burke had capitalised on her status as the only designer producing modern textiles for fashion in Melbourne during the war, and as one of only a few in Australia, yet retailers' acceptance of her furnishing fabrics was uneven. Perhaps furnishing department buyers were hesitant to commit due to wartime conditions. Although Myer began marketing them in 1939, Georges, which had been quick to commission her fashion fabrics, only began stocking Burke's furnishing fabrics after the war. Hicks, Atkinson & Sons, the Collins Street department store described by former Georges visual merchandiser Laurie Carew as 'terribly smart', also began carrying them in the postwar period.[1]

Hicks Atkinson's role as Melbourne's smartest department store was challenged in the late 1930s by Georges' transformation from sales-driven to stylish, achieved by the talented Reta Findlay. Beginning her career as a commercial artist, in 1937 Findlay moved to Georges as advertising manager, but before long directed the buying and all aspects of the store's identity. In her first year she travelled to London and Paris to scope out developments in retail, attend fashion shows and establish relations with European fashion houses; her observations and predictions were broadcast on radio from London. On Findlay's return, Georges' windows were no longer crowded displays filled with price tickets, but became spare modern arrangements characterised by a refined elegance. Under Findlay, Georges' advertising featured sparkling copy, striking illustrations and included Burke's fabrics in seasonal campaigns.

Burke began successfully marketing her textiles in Sydney during the war with leading department store David Jones. Her textiles were shown in the store's 1941 exhibition 'Australian Aboriginal Art and Its Application', a collaboration with the Australian Museum in Sydney. In reviewing the exhibition for *The Sydney Morning Herald*, Paul Haefliger wrote that 'the fabrics of Frances Burke are particularly good'.[2] By 1946 David Jones began promoting her fabrics with advertisements that displayed her name prominently, and in 1948 Burke's latest designs were included in the store's '7 Designers' exhibition, alongside the work of graphic and furniture designer Gordon Andrews, ceramicist Allan Lowe, silversmith James Linton, and furniture designers Stephen Kalmar and George Korody.

A range of Burke's fabrics was sold in Perth at Aherns and Boans department stores, and in Brisbane at Finney Isles department store, the very smart Tritton's, which manufactured its own furniture from 1941, and at Henry Roberts in 1950. While they were exhibited to acclaim in 1941 at Adelaide's Institute Gallery, Burke only secured distribution there after a 1952 exhibition of her work at the Curzon Gallery, which encouraged department store John Martin & Co. to stock them. Burke achieved comprehensive national distribution in the early 1950s. She began selling through stores in Horsham, Victoria; Wagga Wagga, Newcastle and Broken Hill, New South Wales; Mount Gambier, South Australia; Hobart and Burnie, Tasmania; and Ipswich, Queensland.

Advertisements from regional newspapers 1941–54 reveal how Burke's fabrics became widely available during and increasingly after World War II.

Just Opened—
Australian-Made
CHINTZ

Australian-made 36-inch CHINTZ in an entirely new design exclusive to Boans for Western Australia.

Designed by the well-known Australian artist Miss Frances Burke, who received Honourable mention for her work in the Melbourne Exhibition of Commercial Art.

These prints form part of the decorations of the Australian Legation, Washington; Government House, Adelaide; The Aero Club, Canberra; Prince Henry Hospital, Melbourne. Moderately priced at .. .. 8/11 yard. FREIGHT FREE.

FIRST FLOOR

See Display in Boans Murray Street Window.

PAY YOUR HOME THE BEST COMPLIMENT —
GIVE IT
FINE FURNISHINGS!

Chosen for Their Quality and Good Taste

There's nothing to make you so proud of your home as the introduction of bright, modern furnishings.

They bring a new look to your rooms. Choose from Copland's wide selection. Modern Prints by Frances Burke (36in), in bright color combinations at 19/6 yard.

There are floral Cretonnes by such famous makers as Grafton, Duval, Bevis and Sunlover from 9/11 yd.

Laces from 7/6, and Fisher Net from 7/9, are just a few of the special values available.

You'll enjoy looking through the sparkling range, and your home will enjoy the change.

LINOS, FLOOR COVERINGS, PLASTICS
IN A WIDE RANGE

★ MORE FOR YOUR MONEY IN FURNISHINGS AT—
Copland's
FOR SERVICE

Trittons
FURNISHING FABRICS

We're out to win. Fall in and march to Victory with the A.I.F.

All the Latest Radiant Colours and Exquisite Designs for
CURTAINS and LOOSE COVERS
Selection is easy from such a Magnificent Range.

QUALITY VARIETY & VALUE!

These Materials include Burway Hand-printed Fabrics (made in Australia), British Printed Linens, Shadow Tissues, Cretonnes, Cubaleens, Cottage Weaves, Repps, Damasks, Brocades, Chenilles, Muslins, Marquisettes, and Lace Nets.

All designs of Curtains and Loose Covers are made in our own Workroom by a specially selected and expert staff—specialised attention is given to every set ensuring you a highly satisfactory service.

The full-range of famous
FRANCES BURKE
SOFT FURNISHINGS
IS NOW AVAILABLE FROM
FRANK GRIFF'S
Barrier Supply Stores   ★   Argent and Patton Streets

NEW DESIGN AND THE GOOD DESIGN MOVEMENT

In 1947 Burke moved the print works to 46 Hardware Lane, closer to Melbourne's central shopping district and the Myer Emporium, making it a short detour for clients to visit her studio. Within a year the business had expanded to 55 Hardware Lane, taking up the first floor, where Burke established a showroom and retail space.

As an acute businesswoman, Burke decided to respond to the difficult economic conditions of the late 1940s by opening the showroom she named New Design. She complained in 1947 that Japanese printed textiles had been 'dumped' in Australia, forcing her to reduce her staff since her former customers 'were completely stocked with the foreign printed material' and she 'could not hope to compete with the Japanese article, as [its] manufacture was heavily subsidized'.[3] In a later interview Burke reflected on this period after 'the war, when fabrics from all over the world came flooding in, they dropped Australian stuff like a hot brick. I realized for a moment how unfortunate it was to be an Australian in Australia.' Burke 'got over it by opening up her own shop. It was an instant success and her only regret is that she didn't start the shop earlier.'[4]

When opening New Design, Burke's close friend Maie Casey said in her congratulatory speech 'that three things were

Frances Burke fabrics
NEW DESIGN PTY. LTD.

ANNOUNCING THE
OPENING OF OUR
NEW SHOWROOMS
12th APRIL
55 Hardware Street
Melbourne, MU 3571

ARCHITECTURE AND ARTS—APRIL, 1954

New Design at 55 Hardware Lane, formerly Hardware Street, was Burke's first retail venture.

needed for design in industry—faith, enterprise, and imagination and that Frances Burke had all three in good measure'. It was reported that with 'her colourful fabrics draping the wall no other decorations were needed for the warehouse party'.[5] Although Burke hadn't begun to sell furniture or lighting at this stage, a range of locally produced and imported kitchenware items were displayed on locally made tables of tubular steel topped with fashionable new laminates.

At the same time Burke established New Design she positioned herself at the frontline of an evolving campaign for the recognition and celebration of attractive and functional modern design—the Good Design movement. Inspired by the efforts of the British Industrial Design Association, the campaign was led in Australia from 1947 by the Society of Designers for Industry, which Burke was invited to join as a founding member. She spent considerable time and energy from that point forward educating Australian consumers in lectures, writing and interviews to recognise 'good design' and to take pleasure in not only the appearance, but also the usability and safety of local and imported products—like those she thoughtfully sourced and presented in her showroom.

The role of retailer was a logical extension of Burke's work as a designer and was an expression of her philosophy that design should be for everyone, not just an elite. Setting up a retail business was a calculated financial risk, but in doing so she and her staff were able to learn from and integrate the response of a broader range of customers to her product selection and fabric designs. In providing for 'design aware' clients at New Design, Burke recognised an emerging section of the market, which traditional retailers would have viewed as small and financially risky.

Burke's business skills included agility. By 1952 she had moved her printery and relocated her retail business. In the manner of contemporary 'pop-up' shops, Burke's retail business was not only mobile, but co-marketed with Stanley Coe who had operated a retail art gallery and interior design consultancy at 435 Bourke Street since 1949. David Crowther, an associate of Burke's from the textile industry and Royal Melbourne Institute of Technology, observed that she 'was very formidable … she had the talent, the guts and the determination regardless of her sex—those qualities were needed more by a woman than a man in those days … Her business was small enough for her to sell to other retailers, do contract work and become a retailer.'[6]

By diversifying New Design's offerings beyond homewares in the early 1950s, Burke gave exposure to emerging Melbourne designers, with furniture by Grant Featherston and Clement Meadmore and lighting by Meadmore and BECO (Brown Evans & Co.). In the mid-1950s she obtained furniture from the United States by Charles and Ray Eames and Harry Bertoia to use as props for visual merchandising in her shop and for promotional photography. Despite her commitment to supporting local design, Burke also imported American products she felt were necessary for the undersupplied, 'disadvantaged' Australian housewife. These included kettles with insulated handles, ovenproof glass serving dishes and, in an improvement on wooden 'dolly' pegs, spring-loaded clothes pegs.

In 1954 Burke moved the printery to the second floor of 36 Flinders Lane, above wholesalers Jordan and Moss who later picked up her range. She moved New Design yet again, to Little Collins Street and in the coming years would open a separate office–studio at 125 Collins Street. In the early 1960s the office and showroom were relocated to three different addresses in Richmond. While this series of moves suggests a chaotic state of affairs, as a canny businesswoman Burke chose to rent premises for the tax advantage rather than purchase them. Instead she speculated by buying and selling residential property in Anglesea and undertaking a small-scale commercial development in Toorak Road, South Yarra, in addition purchasing the series of homes in East Melbourne where she lived with Chamberlin.

The interior of New Design (c. 1948) by photographer John Warlow showing a range of selected homewares displayed with Burke's fabrics.

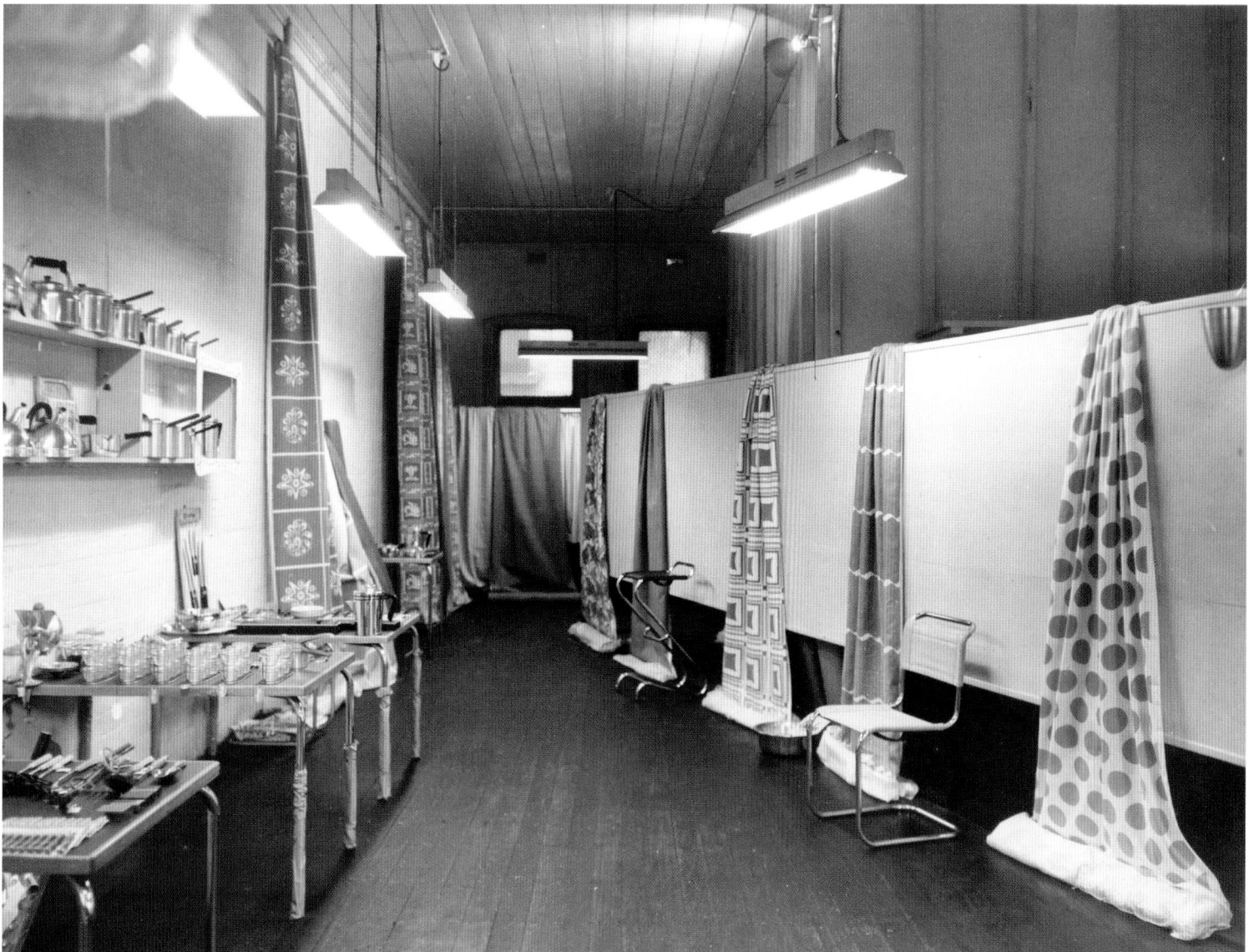

A room setting by Burke from 1954 combining a fibreglass and steel Eames chair imported from the United States,
a lamp by Melbourne designer Clement Meadmore, a locally produced table and a length of Burke's *Surf*.

An advertisement from *Australian House and Garden* from 1953, showing
Burke's marketing of locally designed furniture and furnishings at New Design.

A network of shops

New Design was part of a network of shops, galleries and design consultancies that had developed since the late 1920s in Melbourne's smaller streets and lanes. From 1929 Edith MacMillan's Primrose Pottery Shop was located variously in and near Little Collins Street, stocking the work of local crafts-people including ceramics by the Boyds and Harold Hughan, handwoven fabric from eclarte and handprinted fabric from Michael O'Connell and Lucy Newell.

Fred Ward had opened his eponymous business in early 1932 at 52a Collins Street, accepting commissions for interior design and selling his own furniture, O'Connell fabrics, Navajo blankets, Swedish glass and paintings by local artists. In the following year he moved the business to 367 Little Collins Street, closer to the Primrose Pottery Shop. Ward's gallery manager Cynthia Reed took over in 1934, renaming the business Cynthia Reed Modern Furnishings before leaving for Sydney in early 1935.

Between 1935 and 1938 a small gallery and shop selling fashionable homewares operated in Manchester Lane. Owned by Bob Pulleine, an artist from Adelaide, it sold O'Connell linens and artworks by members of the Group of 12, which included Arnold Shore, Moya Dyring, Clive Stephen and Pulleine himself. The works of artist friends Mary Cecil Allen, Yvonne Atkinson, Russell Drysdale and Peter Purves Smith were also regularly shown.

Many small shops and galleries around Australia disappeared during World War II as both men and women joined the war effort. Wartime rationing in addition to housing and commodity shortages meant there was little to purchase during the war despite the fact that increased employment and war service resulted in many households bringing in two or more salaries, creating unprecedented household savings. As Australians focused on re-establishing their lives after the war, unique small shops made a reappearance, offering appealing furniture and furnishings for the war generation to complete their longed-for new homes.

The re-opening of smaller retailers and galleries was exciting but business conditions were unstable. By 1953 Stanley Coe closed the gallery in Bourke Street he had shared with Burke, and he became a consultant decorator for Princes Gallery, owned by designer Gabrielle Matves, that was located at 52 Collins Street Melbourne. It was a business aiming to display everything 'that goes to make up a good interior, including the work of significant Australian artists … to present the work of talented Australians in a number of fields in an atmosphere more like that of a home than a shop'.[7] It showed the fabrics of Burke, and other textile designers such as Ailsa Graham and John Rodriquez, along with furniture by well-known local designers.

Other significant retailers including Stuart's of South Yarra, established by John Stuart Crowe in 1952, appeared in

An advertisement for Princes Gallery, which sold Burke's fabrics, showing three designs by Ailsa Graham and furniture by Dynametric, a short-lived partnership between designer and store owner Gabrielle Matves and Barrie Paxton.

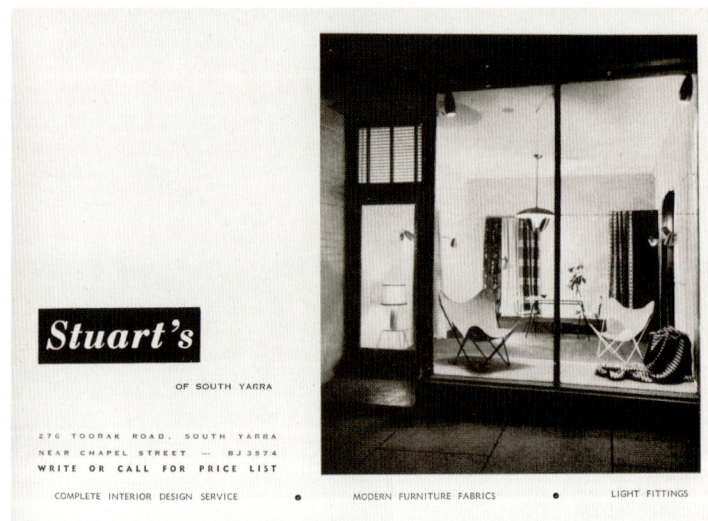

Burke's fabrics displayed with the very popular Butterfly chair, and table and chairs by Clement Meadmore at Stuart's, an interior design consultancy and retailer.

Melbourne suburbs. Stuart's showcased the latest local and international designers' work and trends in its windows facing busy Toorak Road, introducing the public to international design ranges including Knoll and Herman Miller—made in Australia under licence by William Latchford & Sons—that had previously only been seen in magazines. Furniture by local designers including Gerald and Isobel Doubé and Fred Lowen (Fler) was also sold. Burke's fabrics were stocked early on, followed by those of Bee Taplin and Rodriquez.

Ted Worsley, who worked at Stuart's with 'Jack' Crow as a director from 1954, recalled that they 'always hung up a drop of Frances Burke fabrics for ease of understanding the patterns, repeats and scale which was the most important aspect'.[8] From 1959 the two established a second business, Worsley, Crow & Associates, an industrial and interior design consultancy working on commissions for offices, project home interiors,

restaurants and exhibitions, with the furniture, carpets and curtains supplied by Stuart's. These commissions were often initiated by leading Melbourne architects including Robin Boyd and Roy Grounds.

Another successful suburban retailer, Andersons, had been established in the early 1920s. A family-owned and managed furniture manufacturer, wholesaler, retailer and interior design consultancy, by the early 1950s it had stores in seven suburbs and in the regional city of Geelong. Bruce Anderson, a director, had spent time in London working with the Council of Industrial Design and on the 1951 Festival of Britain, which introduced the British public to a new wave of modern design and culture. In addition to specifying Burke fabrics for interiors and using them in their advertisements, under Anderson's management, the store gave active support to local designers of contemporary furniture and lighting.

The Doubé divan in this 1954 advertisement for Andersons is covered in Burke's *Tartan* (1948) while the setting on the top left of the advertisement for Sydney manufacturer Descon has curtains of Burke's *Moresque* (1941).

CONTEMPORARIES: MELBOURNE

When questioned during interviews in the early 1990s, Burke and Chamberlin declined to discuss the concept of competitors, instead describing a number of designers who worked in Melbourne as 'contemporaries'. The list included O'Connell who worked in Melbourne between 1927 and 1937, Graham from 1947 to 1958, Taplin from 1950 to 1962 and Rodriquez from 1950 to 1985. They also mentioned the Sydney studio Annan Fabrics.

Ailsa Graham Art Fabrics

In a 1953 article about Australian furnishing textile design, author Joan Leyser acknowledged Burke's importance:

> The Frances Burke furnishing fabrics were well established in the public esteem long before the import restrictions came into being. The material used is ducks of varying weights, the designs are clear and bold, and the colours are superb. They are particularly suitable for modern furnishings, and will continue to hold ground because of their excellence.[9]

In the same article Leyser presented Ailsa Graham (1925–2015) as the next 'big thing' in the field. While Burke was reluctant to describe Graham as a competitor, it is evident that Graham's business moved into Burke's market using similar motifs.

Graham initially produced small articles with Australiana motifs for the souvenir market, but her business increased significantly from 1951 when Beverley Knox, another Melbourne Technical College (MTC) textile design graduate, joined the staff. The company produced furnishing fabric along with quantities of smaller printed articles. In an interview, Knox explained that nobody 'else in Melbourne except Frances Burke was textile printing in a similar way to ours, and her approach was identifiably her own'.[10] Ailsa Graham Art Fabrics were, in fact, sufficiently similar to Burke's fabrics to have been mistaken by many an unknowing customer. While Graham ran a well-organised business, she did not revive it in 1958 after her factory burnt down.

A 1954 *Australian Home Beautiful* editorial presenting the work of Annan Fabrics of Sydney, Burke, John Rodriquez and Ailsa Graham.

Australian Home Beautiful editorial of 1963 introducing (left to right) *Pierrot* design by Pierrot, *Shadows* by British manufacturer Tennyson as a framed picture, Burke's *Totem* (1948), Melbourne manufacturer Hoad's *Grammercy* and John Rodriquez's *Etruscan*.

STONE AGE LEGENDS in modern design

He tells the tales
of his own people

by Herschell Hurst

WHEN Mr. Bill Onus, of Melbourne, decided to enter the modern furnishing fabric field, he didn't have to stretch his imagination to conjure up designs.

He simply turned to the legendary drawings of his ancestors, transferred them from cave walls to cloth, and produced curtain and furnishing fabrics that are contemporary and original.

The aboriginal legend — yes Bill Onus is an aboriginal — "Churinga" is dramatically told in black drawings on a white 6oz. duck, 36 inches wide.

It is most effective teamed with black wrought-iron furniture.

He has used some of this cloth to cover a magazine shelf under a clear glass-topped black wrought-iron table he has designed. He is printing this design in other colors, too.

Price of this and three other Onus fabrics is about 18/- a yard.

An aboriginal legend is the motif of each of the other fabrics.

Mr Onus has been in the soft-furnishing field for less than two years and already he has a good market in Victoria.

He hopes to be able to increase production within the next year and seek markets in other States.

But under the trade-name "Aboriginal Enterprises" Bill Onus produces many things other than fabrics.

His staff includes artists who do the finished designs from his rough sketches.

These are transferred to boomerangs, scarves, boomerang-shaped coffee tables, stools and pottery.

Under his direction, the artists produce original "genuine Australian" Christmas and greeting cards, each with a hand-painted legendary drawing, with the legend explained inside.

Last year Aboriginal Enterprises made and sold 7000 boomerangs, hundreds of them to tourists from overseas.

His sister-in-law, Mrs. Wynn Onus, is his woodturner. She spends her days over a lathe making delicately balanced boomerangs. She also helps in the printing of the fabrics.

But Mr. Onus is convinced it is in the fabric field he will make his name, and he has his eye on the tourist market for the Olympic Games next year.

Few people know Bill Onus in his role of successful businessman, but most Australians know his name. He is regarded as our champion boomerang thrower. But, more important, the authorities know him as a fighter for his own people.

Mr. Onus is president of the Australian Aborigines' League and a Justice of the Peace. The League secretary is Rev. Doug. Nicholls, a lifelong friend of Bill Onus. They grew up together on the Cummerajunja Mission Station, north of Echuca, on the Murray.

Two and a half years ago Mr. Onus was working as a tally-clerk on the Melbourne wharves.

Not satisfied with his own vast knowledge of the legends of his ancestors, he has read every book on the subject and has spent hours in Sydney's Mitchell Library studying pictures of aboriginal cave drawings.

"Some goods are being sold bearing figures claimed to be aboriginal art, but these are simply what the

designers consider it should be like," he said. "We produce the real thing."

He showed me a beautifully made grass basket. "You mightn't believe this," he said, "but an 80 year old aboriginal woman made that from grass growing round her house at Healesville, Victoria. She uses a big needle made from a Kangeroo's shin bone.

"A wholesaler wanted 200 of these, but I could let him have only two, because she takes a week to make a basket."

* * * *

This is the Onus fabric, called "Churinga."

Here is the "Churinga" legend

In the Dreamtime, at the very beginning, there emerged from Churinga stones (sacred emblems) a man and three women.

Lighting a great fire, the women danced with joyous steps, accompanied by the rhythmical shouts of the man "Wa Wa Wa" . . .

From a great distance a Magpie man was attracted by the sounds. . . . He approached the people and the women encircled him with dancing steps.

Overcome by jealous rage, the man seized a heavy mulga spear and drove the Magpie man away. . . . He changed into a Curlew, as did the women. They flew away. The first man, all alone, also flew away.

Higher and higher they flew, until, overcome by grief and exhaustion, they sank to the ground, where once more they became Churinga stones.

In this day, the Churinga are taken from the sacred hiding place, patterns are drawn on the ground, and men of the Magpie and Curlew totems, with chant and clicking sticks, re-enact in dance the story of their far-off ancestral heroes.

For they believe that they are the reincarnation of these people.

In this 1955 article, Bill Onus argued that objects produced by his business and his Indigenous suppliers were genuine, unlike the work of other (non-Indigenous) designers.

Rodriquez Fabrics

As a young student interested in fabric-printing techniques, John Rodriquez (1928–2000) took Graham's dye chemistry class at MTC and began working with her while he was also employed by émigré designer Gerard Herbst at Prestige Fabrics. Rodriquez later recalled in an interview that he had started Rodriquez Fabrics with

> a couple of one-colour designs, but I tried to use two to three colours so they weren't a replica of Frances, Ailsa also tried to use two to three for the same reason. We started in a big old house in Aspendale, on the beach. On the kitchen table we printed Christmas cards and some placemats; later we moved to Chelsea … In the late fifties we went to Prahran, then South Yarra and then Carlton.[11]

By the time Rodriquez was located in Carlton in the 1960s, he was supplying substantial yardage to the Victorian Hospitals Association in competition with both Burke and Graham, but finding this market crowded, he began supplying the souvenir market. In the early 1960s the potential of the tourist dollar was relatively unrecognised, making this a clever and far-sighted business decision. While Rodriquez retired in 1985, a robust family business continues to operate under his name.

Bill Onus

While not mentioned by Burke as a contemporary in interviews she gave, Bill Onus (1906–1968) ran a studio producing unique handprinted textiles throughout the 1950s. A Wiradjuri man born at Cummeragunja mission in New South Wales, he lived in Melbourne from 1946, engaging in activism as a unionist and member of the Aborigines Progressive Association. In 1952 Onus established Aboriginal Enterprise Novelties, in Belgrave, Victoria, to produce and market boomerangs, woomeras, greeting cards with Aboriginal motifs and textiles informed by the narratives and traditional knowledge of his heritage. Under Onus's direction, the stories and motifs were drawn and developed into accomplished fabric designs by Paula Kerry, a non-Indigenous woman who worked in his studio. Onus's successful business was a forerunner to the Indigenous corporations and collectives producing art, textiles and other crafts in Australia today.

Bee Taplin

Establishing her textile design, fabric and wallpaper printing business in 1950, Bee Taplin (1911–2010) also produced designs on paper, which were sold in the United States, Europe and the United Kingdom. Distributed nationally from Colour Cottage, a retail outlet she opened in Toorak Road, South Yarra, they were designed to match interior paint colours as part of a unified design concept. A business card advertised home visits from 'expert colour consultants and interior decorators who will plan and supply furnishings and floor coverings for individual colour schemes coordinating paints, textures, floor coverings … fabrics … and wallpapers'.

In 1955 Taplin, together with Maurice Holloway, Burke's former partner from Burway Prints, set up Falkiner Fabrics, 'Manufacturers of exclusive furnishing fabrics and Importers of Oriental Wallpapers',[12] to handle the wholesale side of the business. In a brochure she stated rather optimistically that 'the aim of Falkiner fabrics is to anticipate the lines on which Australia's conception of style must progress': Taplin's ideas on modern domestic design and colour replicated those Burke had been promoting for a decade. In 1962 Taplin's interest in painting and exhibiting surpassed her engagement in the textile business and she closed the doors of Falkiner Fabrics.

CONTEMPORARIES: SYDNEY

Sydney also had a lively textile design and print scene, with accomplished designers and printers enjoying a supporting structure of shops, galleries and interior decorators' showrooms that was similar to Melbourne. Some of the shops, including Margo Lewers' Notanda, were clustered on the now demolished Rowe Street in central Sydney.

Margo Lewers

Margo Lewers (1908–1978) established a business in Sydney in 1929 known as the Design Workshop producing her designs for decorative wooden objects and ceramics.[13] Seeking inspiration in 1934, she spent three months studying art and textile design at London's Central School of Arts and Crafts and the summer in Europe. On her return Lewers opened Notanda, a shop selling her own fabric designs and ceramics along with local and imported art and craft work. Despite closing during World War II, Lewers continued to work with a commercial pottery to market her designs in Sydney, Melbourne and various regional centres but ceased producing textiles. An exception was that in 1947, together with her brother, artist Carl Plate, Lewers was invited to contribute to the Modernage range, Claudio Alcorso's project linking selected artists with technicians from his business Silk and Textile Printers to produce startling new fabrics.

Silk and Textile Printers

Established in Rushcutters Bay by Italian Jewish immigrants Claudio Alcorso and Paul Sonnino in 1939, Silk and Textile Printers became a major player in the production of locally designed and screen-printed fabrics. Alcorso discovered that Australia had the highest per capita consumption of dress fabrics in the world, with little local production. The decision to establish the business was made after analysing the potential of the Australian market, and it continued the Alcorso family tradition in the textile industry. As Alcorso later wrote:

> I had been shown samples of fabrics which had been best sellers. But when I went for a swim at Bondi or Manly where my eyes focused on the long-limbed, bronzed women, swimming or sunbaking in a sunlight even stronger than that of my native land, the buyers' examples did not make sense. Looking at the bathers I could visualise them … wearing bold, gay patterns and colours. The buyers were doubtful, some mumbled 'garish' … but they gave us a go. This proved to be one reason for our early success: the younger women liked bolder fashions.[14]

Untitled curtain fabric by Margo Lewers for Notanda.

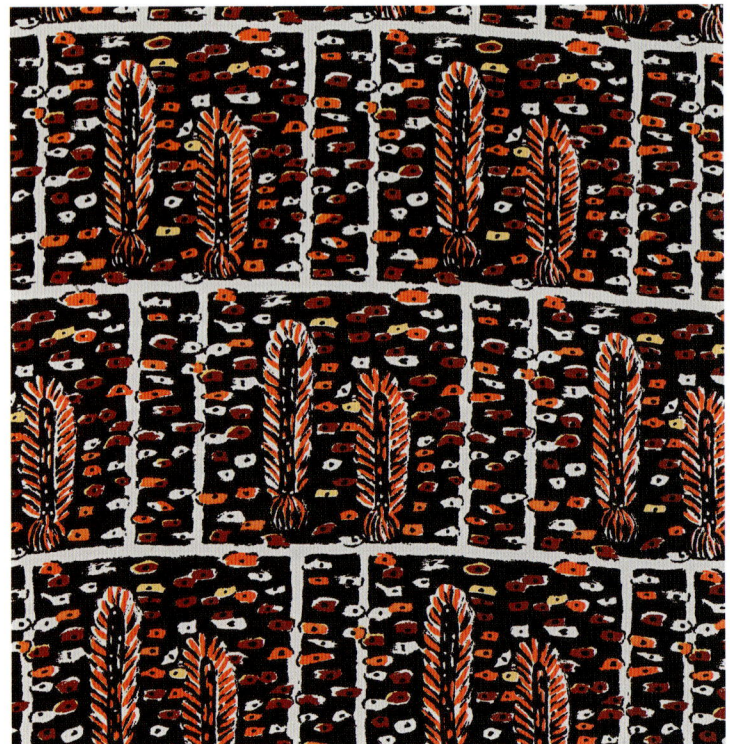

Adina by Margaret Preston for the 1949 Modernage range.

In discussing the early days of the business Alcorso explained, 'There was an emerging Australian culture … and I believed we had a product to command world attention. The war helped to make a leap forward … Prime Minister John Curtin's plea was "To be ready to go ahead to become Australians in truth."'[15] Despite a period of imprisonment during the war as an 'enemy alien', Alcorso was poised to respond to Curtin's words, by contributing to Australian culture and supporting his vision of Australia as an independent nation.

Annan Fabrics

Another Sydney textile design and screen-printing business, Annan Fabrics, also aimed to produce designs reflecting a confident, modern Australia.[16] After establishing the business in Mosman, Sydney, in 1941, Alexandra (Nance) Mackenzie and Anne Outlaw secured a considerable quantity of dyestuff, which enabled them to continue printing designs with two and three colours throughout the war. Germany had been the main international source of dyestuff prior to the outbreak of war, so those needed during the war had to be locally supplied or obtained with great difficulty from Britain. While some have understood the number of colours in their prints as a point of difference between the wartime production of Annan Fabrics and Burke, in fact prior to the war Burke often used only a single colour— it was already a 'hallmark' of her distinctive style.

The company was known for designs inspired by Indigenous culture, notable examples being *Emu Tracks* and *Kangaroo Hunt*. Australian fauna and flora featured along with the exotic plants that flourish in the gardens of Sydney—inspiration for designs such as *Strelitzia*, *Monstera* and *Ginger Plant*. Like Burke, they also produced a range of abstract designs.

Annan Fabrics was similar to Burke's business in many ways. Mackenzie and Outlaw exhibited with the Arts and Crafts Society of New South Wales, and supplied David Jones in Sydney and the Myer Emporium in Melbourne. Like Burke, they treated clients to gallery-style openings, although they didn't extend their offerings to homewares and furniture. Connections made with Sydney architects meant that their textiles appeared in many commercial interiors, including the Wentworth Hotel, the Sydney offices of P&O, Tooth's Brewery, theatres, clubs, universities and schools.[17] Despite the quality of their work, Annan Fabrics suffered from the challenge posed by local and international competition, and the partnership dissolved in 1954 following the bankruptcy of a major customer.

Banksia by Annan Fabrics.

INFLUENTIAL INTERIOR DESIGNERS AND DECORATORS

Although Burke retailed her own fabrics, supplied furniture stores, department stores and a range of interior design consultancies in Melbourne, her national profile benefitted from the support of a group of significant interior designers and decorators in Sydney. Their work was promoted through newspapers and magazines, including Australia's most fashionable publication of the 1930s and 1940s, *The Home*. Burke considered interior decorator Margaret Lord and designer Marion Hall Best as being important for her business in specifying her fabrics, selling them and promoting modern design in Australia. Discerning interior decorator Molly Grey was another early champion of Burke's work.

Molly Grey

After training in the United States and Europe, Molly Grey arrived back in Sydney, where she found work as an in-house designer at David Jones in 1934. The next year she hosted a radio program on 2FC titled *Let's Do Up the House*.[18] For an article titled 'Wartime Furnishing in Australia', Grey chose to feature a Sydney living room with curtains in a striking Burke fabric, *Canna Leaf* (1940) in 'burnt sugar and aquamarine'.[19] The room's furnishings and accessories, which were produced by Australian designers, included a chair and sofa covers upholstered in an aquamarine colour, chosen to team with Burke's fabric.

Margaret Lord

Interior designer, lecturer, broadcaster and writer Margaret Lord (1908–1976) had a training paralleling Burke's. Starting in Melbourne she studied for three years at the Swinburne Technical College's School of Art before taking night classes at the Gallery School and attending the George Bell School. Since there was no local training course for interior decorators she travelled to London in 1936, enrolling at the Central School of Arts and Crafts before landing a job at the fashionable interior design consultancy Reens Arta. Later she taught at the prestigious Arnold School of Interior Decoration, becoming the school's director of studies.

Returning to Australia in 1940, Lord based herself in Sydney, where she believed there were more opportunities than in Melbourne.[20] She lectured for the YWCA and for the ABC in its 1941 *Design in Everyday Things* radio series; leading to a commission from the Australian Army to create and teach a correspondence course for servicemen and women. The course informed a 1944 textbook *Interior Decoration: A Guide to Furnishing the Australian Home*, the first significant Australian guide to the practical aspects of designing and furnishing

A 1940 interior by Molly Grey featuring Burke's *Canna Leaf* design.

A two-colour version of Burke's *Canna Leaf* (1940) in Margaret Lord's 1944 book *Interior Decoration: A Guide to Furnishing the Australian Home*, illustrated by Elaine Haxton.

The 1946 apartment of Viennese designer Frederick Sterne, utilising Burke's *Crete* design, appeared in more than one local magazine. After emigrating in 1938, Sterne worked for architectural practice Leighton Irwin before setting up the Melbourne Technical College's three-year Interior Design Diploma in 1948.

An accomplished use of two different Burke designs in three colourways, contrasting with a vibrant feature wall and dark-toned upholstery by Marion Hall Best at St Andrews College, University of Sydney.

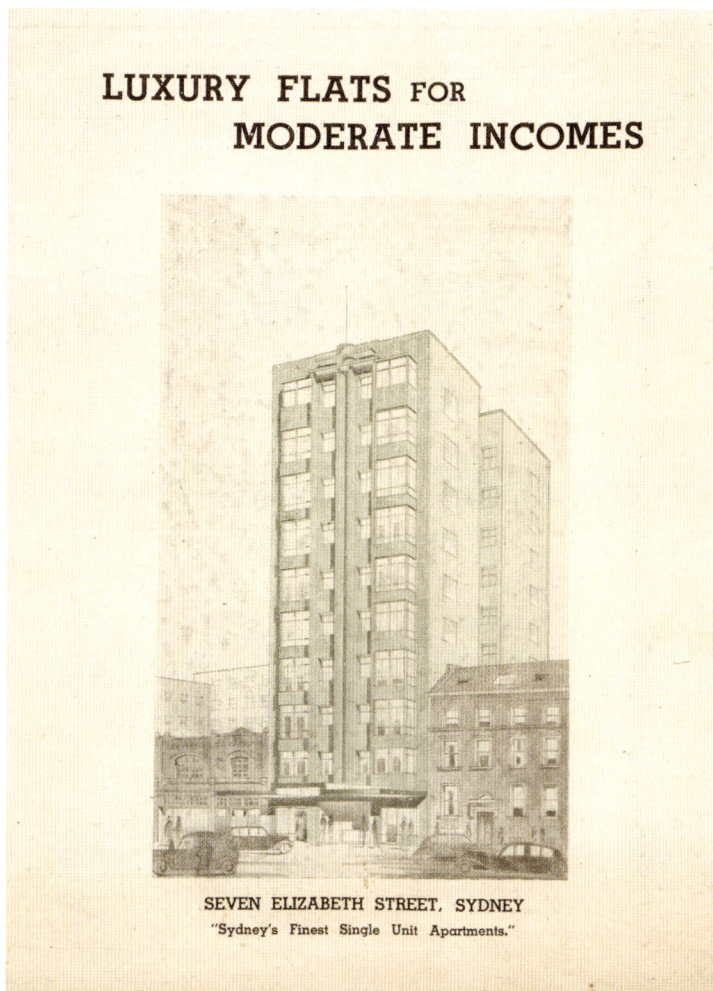

LUXURY FLATS FOR MODERATE INCOMES

SEVEN ELIZABETH STREET, SYDNEY
"Sydney's Finest Single Unit Apartments."

Marion Hall Best designed fifty fully furnished apartments at 7 Elizabeth Street, Sydney, described by a sales brochure as 'luxury flats for moderate incomes'. Hall Best later wrote, 'It was here that Frances Burke's materials made their first appearance in Sydney. They were a sensational success.'[21]

a modern home, which included a clear reference to Burke's fabrics without mention of her name.[22] Lord established her interior decoration practice with a commission for a new Sydney University Union Building, where she combined Burke's hand-printed curtains with 'modern furniture in woods of natural colour and finish, upholstery in a combination of coloured hides and textured weaves … Everything … was Australian and the effect was fresh and youthful'.[23]

Ambitious, stylish and well-connected, Lord's profile grew in the postwar period. A much-cited expert on interior decoration and a founding member of the New South Wales chapter of the Society of Interior Designers, she also became a colour consultant for the Berger Paint company. Lord was commissioned to design factory and office interiors for companies including Shell, Wrigley's, and Johnston & Johnston, and she continued choosing Burke's fabrics in her postwar work.

Marion Hall Best

Gifted colourist, designer and communicator, Marion Hall Best (1905–1988) was Australia's leading postwar interior designer. She commenced practising in 1935 and established her eponymous showroom in Woollahra, Sydney, in 1938 stating it was 'the time to prove the value of the artist to industry in creating new areas of good design'.[24] From the inception of her business, Hall Best promoted Australian furnishing fabrics and was quick to use and retail Burke's. 'She was proud of introducing innovative Melbourne artists to Sydney, particularly the textile designer Frances Burke … with whom she collaborated during the lean war years and into the 1950s.'[25]

Hall Best used Burke's designs for three notable projects in collaboration with émigré architect Emil Sodersten: apartments at 7 Elizabeth Street, Sydney, in 1940; Peter Playfair's flat in Birtley Towers in 1953; and St Andrew's College, University of Sydney, in 1956. In an unpublished memoir, Hall Best described the Elizabeth Street apartments: 'the colour schemes were sophisticated … The fabrics were all wash[able]—plain coarse linens, "Frances Burke" handprinted, fast colours on white duck in first rate design'.[26]

Evolving into a highly sophisticated designer, Hall Best selected Burke's and other locally produced fabrics and furniture to create the striking modern interiors for which she became renowned. During World War II she established a separate studio to print the designs of her sister Dora Sweetapple and other local artists. After the war Hall Best also imported outstanding international furniture and fabrics for her showrooms. According to gallery director and art historian Daniel Thomas, 'Marion Best was neither an Australian chauvinist, nor a British colonial, nor a victim of post war cultural imperialism or Eastern hippy exotica. Hers was a true internationalism, in which Australia took its place with confidence and ease.'[27]

Marion Hall Best's showroom in the early 1950s, incorporating a Grant Featherston Relaxation range chair, a Clement Meadmore standard lamp and three Burke fabrics: *Wavy Stripe*, *Squares* and *Drum*.

The striking dining alcove in an apartment designed by Marion Hall Best for Peter Playfair in 1953, using *Tiger Stripe* (1938) in charcoal and *Polka Dot* in green with contrasting cushions and 'canopy'.

The original caption for this image read: 'Fashions made in Australia for this Olympic summer. Photographed in a beautiful terraced garden, typical of many Australian homes … Blue cotton, magnolia printed dress with unbelted slenderness and back buttoning jacket.'

A 1961 streetscape of Flinders Lane, Melbourne, when it was the centre of the Australian rag trade.

FABRICS FOR FASHION

While Burke had begun her business producing beach and resort-wear fabrics for Georges and Myer, in early 1938 she made clear that she was planning to focus on producing furnishing fabrics.[28] Initially this was to keep production going through Melbourne's cooler months, when cotton and linen were not worn, and to allow her to develop designs on a larger scale. The fact that furnishing fabrics had a longer cycle would have appealed to her business sense.

Throughout the Depression of the 1930s Australian home dressmakers often used furnishing fabrics for clothing as part of the 'make do and mend' ethos. From her studio during World War II, in addition to lightweight cotton and rayon dress lengths, Burke sold hemmed pieces of furnishing fabric that women could use to create fashionable garments. Despite specialising in furnishings in the postwar period, Burke continued printing a limited range of fashion fabrics.

Advertising for the 1955 summer collection of Lana Styles, a Flinders Lane fashion business, suggested that wholesalers Jordan and Moss had begun successfully marketing Burke's designs to fashion manufacturers. A newspaper article announcing that 'Well-known Melbourne designer Frances Burke has now turned her originality from furnishing fabrics to dress materials with an equal measure of success' conveyed a selective amnesia. The business claimed it had secured exclusive rights to manufacture clothing in selected fabrics, including Aboriginal-influenced, nautical and geometrical designs.[29] That claim of exclusivity didn't preclude the use of Burke's *Magnolia* design for a dramatic fitted dress and unusual back-fastening jacket by another Melbourne label, Shirtmakers Sportswear, in the same

year. Photographed by Helmut Newton for the first Australian Fashion Supplement of British *Vogue*, Burke would have been delighted that the stylishness of this design, which had continued to evolve from the late 1930s, was considered fashionable twenty years later.

Another fashion label employing Burke's fabrics was the chic and expensive Magg boutique, owned from 1946 to 1976 by (Dame) Zara Holt, wife of Harold Holt, Prime Minister of Australia. Holt's early business partner was (Lady) Betty Grounds, wife of architect Roy Grounds. According to Fabie Chamberlin, Zara preferred Burke's plain dyed rather than printed fabrics, in particular Bad Black, Potato and Jade.[30] Grounds recalled that plain coloured fabrics in Bad Black and Schiaparelli Pink were often ordered for Magg.[31]

Genevieve Lansell, niece of Zara Holt, recalled the ways her aunt used Burke's fabrics in her range in the early 1950s:

> I picked up the fabrics from the showroom in Hardware Street [now Lane]—15 yards of heavy fabric wrapped in brown paper … catching the tram back to Magg on Toorak Road in Toorak village. Aunty Zara made shorts, wraparound skirts and strapless tops which tucked into the skirts. We couldn't wait to have Frances Burke shorts for the beach—we all *loved* the yellow and the coral colours. We all had bright pink Frances Burke skirts … it was furnishing fabric. They had waistbands—full skirts cut on the cross with hand-rolled hems.[32]

Evidently Holt found Burke's crisp furnishing-weight cottons in vibrant colours perfect for casual clothes and resort wear.

An example of an overseas label using Burke's fabric remarkably came to light in 2019 when the Victoria & Albert Museum, London, displayed a garment from a private collection. London designer Mary Quant produced the simple, light cotton summer blouse printed with Burke's *Goanna* design in 1957. Displayed early one morning in the window of Bazaar, her trendsetting boutique in bohemian Chelsea, it was purchased almost immediately by Caroline Hooper, a student who recalled being eager to impress her geologist boyfriend who was returning after three years working in Antarctica. Hooper reported the early sale of the eye-catching hot pink blouse was to the shop assistant's consternation, as Quant was having trouble keeping the window freshly supplied with new

garments and would sometimes sell out of garments before closing for the day.

It is not clear where Quant sourced this fabric and whether this was a one-off piece. While Burke may have presented fabric samples when she travelled to London in 1953, there is no record of her ever having established a relationship with a British distributor. Another possibility is that when Donald Tomlinson from the Manchester Cotton Board travelled to Melbourne in 1954 researching Australian printed cottons, he obtained a sample. After being used in an exhibition in Manchester and to illustrate an article in the British journal *Design*, it is possible that it was later sold as a remnant.

The vibrant colours and strong graphic designs of Burke's fabrics were also valued by home dressmakers of the 1950s and 1960s. Young Melbourne draughtswoman Beverley Ednie,

Caroline Hooper was dressed to impress in her Mary Quant blouse made with Burke's *Goanna* fabric in 1957.

On her honeymoon at Cowes, Philip Island, in 1954, Beverley Ednie wearing a blouse and skirt of slate-blue in an untitled design.

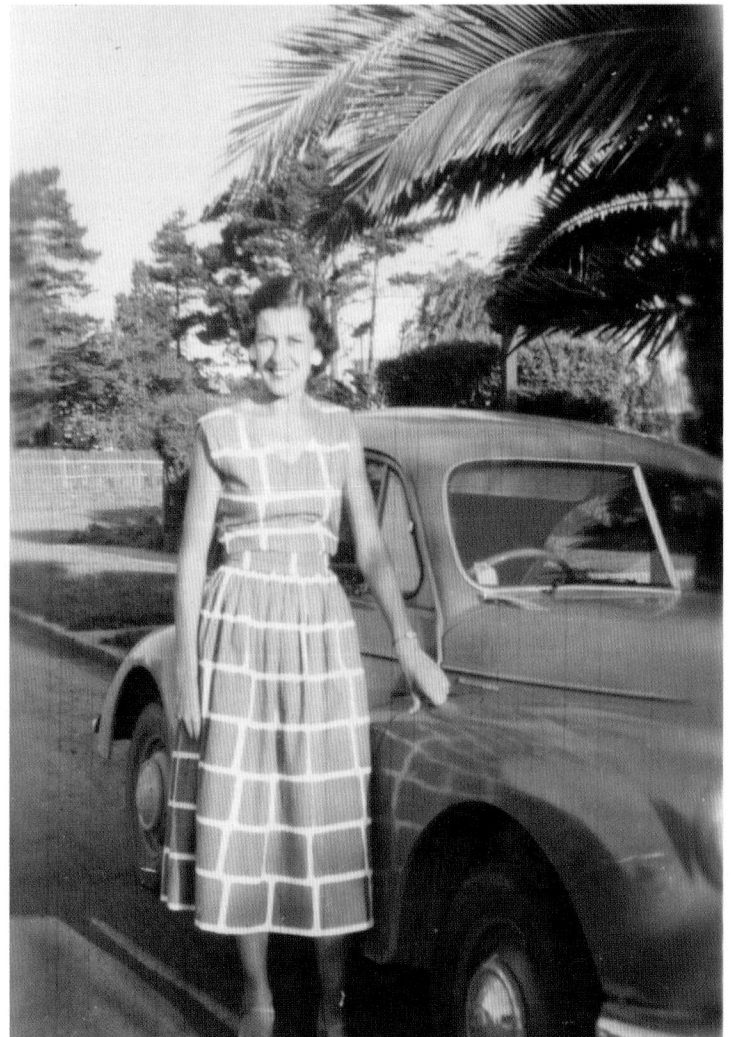

for example, purchased Burke's fabrics to make clothing for her honeymoon. A later photograph shows her wearing a sundress in Burke fabric outside the home she and husband Ian commissioned from architect Robin Boyd. They bought Meadmore chairs and a table, and BECO lighting but due to an unexpected 'blow-out' in the architect's fee, Ednie had been unable to complete the interior with the curtains in Burke's fabrics as she had planned.[33]

Doubtless there were many other stylish women who purchased Burke's fabrics to make striking garments. Museum collections of Burke's fabrics reveal that she continued to print a limited range of lighter-weight fashion fabrics in cotton, rayon and other synthetics into the mid-1960s, and in a unique case printed on wool for the Dina fashion label.

Beverley in another outfit from her trousseau—a dress in *Tartan* in blue and green, cleverly cut on the diagonal. A double exposure, the photograph also shows her husband Ian.

Pregnant with her eldest child, Beverley wearing a casual shift made using Burke's *Tiger Stripe* in a bright yellow print on white.

Nautical and aeronautical designs

The popularity of cruises for the middle-class market not only stimulated interest in Pacific motifs, it also encouraged the use of nautical themes in Australian women's fashions. In the 1920s Coco Chanel had cleverly analysed the fabrics, colours and trimming of nautical clothing worn by the crew and wealthy owners of yachts sailed during the fashionable summer seasons in Europe and the United Kingdom. Applying them to resort wear for her wealthy female clients, Chanel created a sporty, slightly androgynous look by the standards of the times, establishing a precedent that has impacted mainstream fashion and furnishings from the 1930s onwards.

Since supplying fabrics for beach and resort wear was the main impetus behind Burke's early commissions from the late 1930s for Georges department store and the Myer Emporium, she picked up on the nautical theme, producing a number of designs using navy blue on cream or white, with motifs inspired by boats and sailing. *Anchor* (c. 1939) featured the motif with interwoven arabesques of chain and *Yacht Race* (1939) depicted a sleek contemporary craft viewed from a dynamic overhead viewpoint, cutting diagonally through a deep blue sea, interspersed with wheel and anchor motifs. Another nautical design, *Rope and Shell* (1939), was commissioned by architect Brian O'Rorke along with a mural by Douglas Annand for the dining room of the elegant Orient Line building in Spring Street, Sydney, in 1939–40.

While women had been involved in aviation since the contribution of Katharine Wright to the earliest successful flying machines built by her brothers, the availability of surplus and decommissioned airplanes after World War I gave increasing numbers of women the chance to fly. In Australia, the face of female aviation was the glamorous, approachable Nancy Bird Walton, who at nineteen had been the youngest Australian woman to gain a commercial pilot's licence. Taught by pioneer aviator Charles Kingsford Smith, she became a long-distance race winner and pilot for the first flying medical service for outback New South Wales and Queensland in 1935.

Burke's close friend and supporter Maie Casey took up flying in 1938 after her husband purchased a yellow Percival Vega Gull aircraft and laid out an airstrip at their family property Edrington, at Berwick in Victoria. Curtains for the plane were supplied by Burke, made up in *Windsock* (1940) fabric featuring motifs of the device informing pilots of the prevailing wind. *Speedbird* (1959) was another aeronautical design from a later period; it may have been a commission for British Airways, as it replicated the company's visual identity. A third aeronautical design, not found in any public collections, was commissioned by Roma Barlow, the wife of a commercial pilot of Douglas aircraft. In honour of her husband's career, or perhaps as a playful slap on the wrist for his inattention, she asked Burke to produce a design illustrating the airplane to be made into a bathing suit that she wore on the beach in fashionable Portsea in the summer of 1938.[34]

Anchor (c. 1939)

Yacht Race (1939)

Rope and Shell (1939)

Barnacle Bill (1937)

Windsock (1940)

4

CREATING THE FRANCES BURKE BRAND

Portrait of a bright and cheerful-looking Burke in her studio in the 1950s.

This blue and yellow version of *Wuramu* is from the collection of the National Gallery of Australia, Canberra. Another colourway offered was black and brown.

Frances Burke's story is about a talented creative who moved from painting and drawing to fabric design and printing. It is also the story of a fiercely independent woman who was determined to build a successful business, one that would allow her to share her creativity with a broader public. To build and maintain a market for her fabrics, Burke undertook a number of steps that we would now describe as a brand strategy. Although she lacked any kind of business training apart from a brief stint in the advertising agency Catts-Patterson, Burke was sufficiently savvy and ambitious to create a range of opportunities for her business based on her identity as a creative individual who could skilfully communicate her ideas about design.

Design historian Michael Bogle suggests that to better understand postwar design, the 'establishing of milieu … an understanding of the social setting [has] become essential for appraisal of this rich period'.[1] Burke's education at the Melbourne Technical College (MTC), the Gallery School and the George Bell School meant she was part of a coterie of artists and designers. After establishing her business, Burke would have become aware that a wider circle would help build her profile and hopefully expand her market. She extended her circle by joining the Victorian Arts and Crafts Society, and attending gallery openings and theatre first nights, and hosting dinners for friends and acquaintances.

Following the practice of many design-related businesses of the interwar period, Burke chose personalisation as her brand strategy. While initially registered as Burway Prints in 1937 (combining the names Burke and Holloway), there was little mention of Maurice Holloway in interviews. When he withdrew from the business in 1942, publicity continued to focus on Burke rather than her newly registered business partner Jane Williams, or on Chamberlin when she joined in 1948. In addition to promoting the textiles under the name Frances Burke from 1937, most of her designs eventually displayed her signature in various formats on the selvedge. The name Frances Burke Fabrics was used in advertising and widely recognised although not officially registered.

After World War II Burke began to travel overseas and establish her reputation as an expert on design, especially in relation to the home, adding a further dimension to the personalisation of her brand. In addition to giving interviews before and after her trips abroad, from 1950 Burke began giving lectures and, from 1954, writing for a range of publications. These activities broadened public interest in her fabrics and her retail ventures, consolidating her reputation as an expert on design and as a modern tastemaker. In addition to her own advertising and communications, Burke's fabrics appeared in numerous product advertisements in the 1950s and 1960s, where they were used as visual shorthand, communicating a market positioning, a contemporary product or service.

Just as the AWA radio was 'modern and attractive in design' in 1949, so too were the curtains in Burke's *Wuramu*.[2]

"TOTEM" a Frances Burke reg UNIT COLOR DESIGN

a "Frances Burke" reg design · pure cotton.

"RANGGA" a Frances Burke DESIGN

STACCATO" a "Frances Burke" UNIT COLOR DESIGN

Examples of some of the selvedge marks that Burke used at various stages in her business. The term 'Unit Colour Design' was first used in 1958 to market a group of designs, while other marks noted whether a design was registered for copyright and the kind of base fabric used.

PRODUCT BRANDING: SELVEDGE MARKS

Probably one of the most effective means of profile-raising—positioning, promoting and marketing—over the duration of Burke's business was her use of selvedge marks. By the mid-1940s Burke had personalised her product, inserting variations of her crisp, easily read signature and business name as the identifying mark, 'protecting' her designs against either lack of recognition or, more distressingly, false attribution. She complained that her designs were copied and that she was unable to prevent copyright infringement.[3]

In 1953 and 1954 Burke, at a cost of two pounds each, registered eleven designs, most probably on advice from lawyers. A few of these designs appeared in magazines, but it remains a mystery why particular designs were selected in this process. Registrations of two popular designs were renewed for an additional five years: *Goanna* through to 1963 and *Shields* to 1964; however, the remainder were not renewed, and no new designs were registered.

Increasingly Burke changed the information provided in the selvedge marks. To date, thirteen different versions have been identified. In effect Burke saw the selvedge mark on a fabric as her 'brand promise'—communicating to her current and potential clients that hers was a quality imprint on a quality base fabric that they could trust to be washing and light fast. Frances Burke fabrics stood for quality in the marketplace.

THE ARTS AND CRAFTS SOCIETY

Founded in 1908, the Victorian Arts and Crafts Society was established by a small group of people, predominantly technical educators and successful architects including WAM Blackett and Marcus Martin. The society 'emphasized the values of good design and the use of appropriate motifs and materials'.[4] 'Appropriate motifs' meant appropriate to the function of the object, such as using wheat to decorate a bread crock, but also that the motif should be relevant to place. In the Australian context this meant using local native flora such as waratahs and flannel flowers with fauna such as possums or kangaroos.

Membership of the society gave Burke the chance to test the market and to obtain early feedback on her choices of colour and design, both through sales in the society shop and generous press coverage of its regular exhibitions. She gained significant publicity in this way; as one of three new members of the society in 1938, Burke was mentioned in no less than eight reviews and articles. The author of a review in *The Age* on 26 March explained:

> She is very keen on using the Australian flowers in her work as much as possible, and her idea is to create a demand for Australian flora and make it known, particularly overseas, in all varieties of designs. The linens are modern, but not eccentric, and the flower patterns, some of them rather conventionalized, are distinct and unusual. After all, we are Australians, so why not have our own native designs, especially when they are so attractive, in our homes?[5]

While in the early 1930s the society was criticised for having the air of a genteel ladies' club, it underwent an evolutionary process in the following decades, broadening the membership by inviting applications from recently arrived European émigrés with craft skills.

The active involvement of architects in the society and its role in espousing good design in Melbourne exerted a profound and guiding influence, laying the foundations of Burke's thinking. The influence of the society on Burke and the connections she made through it should not be underestimated, and she remained an active member throughout her career, continuing into the exciting years of the craft revival in the late 1960s and 1970s. A review of the society's biannual exhibition in October 1965 reported that 'Frances Burke's finely controlled backdrop curtain design was as always a striking virtuoso display of sophisticated colour'.[6]

27.II.40

My dear Frances,

How are you ?

The time has come when I can no longer endure the squalor of
my immediate surroundings, so please decorate my Sixteen yards of
sateen that you have from Riddell's with the fern frond pattern in
the colour ~~Iesnelse~~ enclose. I had induced the landlord , for his
own pride to repaint the dining room , which was rather grim, and it
is being done in a nice Chinese sort of yellow, agaist which the
enclosed green looks well.   The Trustees Executors Co 40I, Collins St
General Manager Sydney Jones, will fix up the printing costs and freight
with you, if you show them this letter.   I think , for a dining room
that the sateen would look better than the linen, and if you can do it
I would like the green exactly as this pattern.   Did you ever get a
letter from me making a plea for luncheon mats of Australian design.
 (Not gum nuts and boomerangs!)   No more now as I want this to catch the
mail,   Love from

maie Casey

Mrs R.G. Casey
Fern Leaf
Satten 13.1.41

A letter from Maie Casey to Burke with a strip of fabric showing the colour Casey had
selected for the Australian legation dining room in Washington, DC.

The *Lyrebird* placemat designed for the dining room table to be used for working lunches at the Australian legation.

MAIE CASEY: AN INFLUENTIAL PATRON

Another significant source of support for Burke was her friendship with society livewire and patron Maie Casey, who provided her with an expanded milieu and considerable publicity. According to author Philip Jones, 'Maie … was her best friend and this gave her great cachet.'[7] In addition to catching up at George Bell's Thursday Club, Burke and Casey painted together and attended gallery openings. Burke and Chamberlin were invited to dinners at the Caseys' Melbourne pied-à-terre. With their mutual love of the arts, their energetic pursuit of personal goals and their enthusiasm for mixing with others who were achieving professional success, Casey and Burke shared some remarkably similar traits despite their very different social backgrounds and a ten-year difference in their ages. Casey's confident sense of command and adventurous spirit were qualities that Burke would have admired and sought to emulate.

When Casey and husband Richard spent time in London on a diplomatic posting during the 1920s, she took the opportunity to enrol at the Westminster School of Art. They returned to Australia in 1931 so that he could stand as a United Australia Party candidate, bringing with them modern rugs and the first tubular steel furniture seen in Australia. Recognised as a woman of taste, Casey was an important early patron of Fred Ward, using his furniture in their house at Duntroon, Canberra, where they lived from 1932 to 1934 and later at Little Parndon, their pied-à-terre in East Melbourne.

During Casey's tenure as the House of Representatives member for Corio, assistant treasurer from 1933 to 1934,

treasurer from 1935 to 1938 and minister for supply and development in 1939, the couple regularly flew themselves between Canberra and their country house near Harkaway, Victoria. Canberra Aero Club's commission for Burke to design curtains for its clubhouse (probably *Windsock*) in the late 1930s was likely made on the advice of Casey, since she and Richard were keen pilots and members of the club. When Australia entered World War II in 1939, Richard was appointed Australia's first ambassador to the United States, making him responsible for establishing and managing Australia's relationship with the United States at a crucial time.

The Caseys' departure for Washington was recorded in *The Herald*:

> Mrs Casey is taking with her a number of Miss Frances Burke's designs for hand printed linen, satin and chintz. The colour and design for the furnishings will be placed on order here after Mrs Casey has become accustomed to the climate, circumstances and conditions in Washington.[8]

When Casey was interviewed about the importance of their roles in Washington, DC, for *Australia: National Journal* in late 1939, she was clear that part of her role was to ensure that the Australian legation was as 'Australian' as possible. For the rented American Colonial–style red-brick home Casey and her husband were to live in, she ordered Burke's *Fern* in green for the sateen

Australian artist Mary Cecil Allen's *Kangaroo*, a dramatic 1.8-metre high screen, was commissioned by Maie Casey from New York–based Allen. When Casey's private secretary Pat Jarrett accompanied Allen to the Bronx Park Zoo to make preparatory sketches, they saw 'a big red kangaroo standing in the middle of the herd. Mary decided he must go in the middle of the group on her screen, because of his magnificent colour.'[9]

Richard and Maie Casey photographed in Calcutta (1944) by Cecil Beaton when serving as viceroy and vicereine of Bengal, the representatives of King George VI. Maie was wearing a suit made in a design Burke titled *Bengal Tiger*—it was a great talking point when worn on her extensive travels around Bengal and for diplomatic occasions.

curtains of the dining room and commissioned Burke to create placemats and napkins with the instruction: no penguins or koalas! The room also featured a specially commissioned screen entitled *Kangaroo,* which was painted by Mary Cecil Allen, a fellow George Bell student and a great friend of both Casey and Burke, who was then living in New York. Casey ensured that the modern art and design she introduced to the legation gained press coverage both in the interests of her husband's career and for the artists and designers whose work she championed.

An article in *Australian Woman's World* presented Burke's commission for the legation as proof of her work having 'a particularly national character':

> When Mrs R G Casey, the wife of the Australian Minister in Washington chose some of them to take to America to furnish her new home there, it was probably as much because they would serve as a vivid recollection of her own country as because she would be proud to exhibit them there as the work of an Australian.[10]

As a result of World War II, Burke's Arts and Crafts–influenced designs of native flora and fauna were re-cast as expressing national pride, rather than being the 'appropriate ornament' of local significance that the Arts and Crafts movement promoted. In a 1941 advertisement for Burke's fabrics at Boans department store in Perth, the designs were promoted as forming 'part of the decorations of the Australian legation, Washington; Government House, Adelaide; the Aero Club, Canberra',[11] indicating that Casey's patronage had enabled Burke to represent her country.

Richard was appointed British minister of state in Cairo in 1942, where his diplomatic skills combined with his wife's lively intelligence and application to her diplomatic duties were so impressive that in late 1943 Winston Churchill appointed them as viceroy and vicereine of Bengal. Around this time Casey commissioned dress fabric from Burke, who developed a flowing design appropriately titled *Bengal Tiger,* showing the creature gliding through a leafy jungle. Various photographs taken by Cecil Beaton in 1944 around Government House, Calcutta, include Casey looking very stylish and making a diplomatic statement in a dress and jacket celebrating Bengal's natural heritage.

In 1965, after a distinguished political career, Lord Casey was appointed governor-general of Australia. In the four years they spent at Government House (Yarralumla) in Canberra, Maie Casey 'converted [it] into a salon for artists, musicians and writers while dutifully entertaining the dignitaries who came with the job'.[12] She commissioned two sets of curtains from Burke, one in a design titled *Regency Stripe* and another in a textured stripe titled *Zen.*

BURKE'S WAR EFFORT

Burke made a direct contribution to the war effort in 1940, offering to screen print the defence authorities' recruitment and anti-gossip-themed posters. Students at MTC, Swinburne Technical College and Caulfield Technical School, along with twenty commercial and fine artists, submitted designs for an exhibition at Myer Emporium's Mural Hall, from which four were selected. At that time the Defence Department also accepted 500 copies of a poster designed and printed by Frances Burke, showing 'a finger across a woman's mouth—don't talk you don't know who the enemy is'.[13]

The Commonwealth Government's World War II propaganda effort included encouraging the public to think about and plan the kind of life they wanted to live after the war. Two series of recorded talks titled 'Design in Everyday Things' that were 'specially designed to provoke thought and discussion amongst listeners' were broadcast by the Australian Broadcasting Commission (ABC) in 1941.[14] They covered topics related to design, from city planning to interiors and clothing. Leading designers were sought out to take part and an informative 100-page book was published by the ABC with 'outlines' of the talks and illustrations. Clearly it was well conceived and well received, with Bogle noting that 'The authoritativeness of the broadcast, the prestige of its participants … seem to have initiated much of the design debate during the war years'.[15] While Burke was not one of the speakers, interior decorator Margaret Lord gave two of the talks and likely referred to Burke's fabrics as exemplary Australian design.

A rare photograph of Maurice Holloway in the Burway studio. The caption in the ABC booklet suggests that interior decorator Margaret Lord discussed Burway fabrics, some of which were hung for this photograph: left to right, *Jungle*, *Windsock*, *Snake and Dugong*, *Speedbird* and *Yacht Race*.

DESIGNING FOR THEATRE

Burke began working with the Little Theatre in South Yarra, bringing her designs to a new audience in 1946. Irene Mitchell, who was the manager, producer and director, was part of Burke's milieu, and organised a busy schedule for the repertory theatre. This included some plays performed at Melbourne's revered Princess Theatre and a touring program that was taken to regional cities and towns.[16] Burke's first set design was for *Enduring as the Camphor Tree,* by prolific Australian playwright Russell Oakes, described as 'a play in the old Chinese manner'.[17] One of the lead actors was twenty-year-old Frank Thring, who had trained at Mitchell's Academy of Dramatic Art. While Burke painted the sets, the vintage costumes—originally created for performances of Chinese opera—were borrowed from the Bendigo Chinese Association. In a 1952 revival the sets were recycled, while the costumes were designed by Mitchell and made up in Burke's fabrics. Three years after her first foray into theatre, Burke designed sets for another Little Theatre production, an Irish play called *Happy as Larry.*

In 1951, five years after he starred in *Enduring as the Camphor Tree*, Thring took over a building that housed the Melbourne Repertory Theatre at 3 Armstrong Street, Middle Park, renaming it the Arrow Theatre. Inspired by his father's achievements as a theatrical and film entrepreneur, and bankrolled by his mother, Thring formed a plan to stage sophisticated productions for a more discerning audience than he perceived the Little Theatre had attracted. Burke was commissioned to transform the Arrow Theatre into a place that fashionable Melbourne would rush to visit. Her 'unprecedented colour scheme' was much admired:

> As usual Frances has used colour boldly and effectively. In the foyer lavender blue, pale grey and chartreuse are skilfully blended—and curtains provide a clever camouflage to awkward corners. In the auditorium itself a wall of shocking-pink contrasts with two, curtain-draped walls of chartreuse while proscenium and stage curtains are of junior navy blue and white.[18]

It was reported that 'Mrs Olive Thring, mother of the director, wore a deep blue taffeta gown with chartreuse accents in exactly the tones of the Arrow décor'.[19] Alternatively, the rambunctious Mrs Thring could have chosen Burke's other highlight colour, the spectacular Schiaparelli (shocking) Pink, which may have been more in character. The critic for the *Port Phillip Gazette*, JWK, 'found the colour scheme "rather alarming", but symptomatic of the "new lease of life" that had been given to the old place'.[20]

Comedian Barry Humphries recalled that as a teenager he was part of the alternative 'Push', which met at Thring's haven for their jazz nights in the early 1950s; exposure to Burke's exciting use of colour was experienced by 'long haired youths in suede shoes and corduroy trousers … women who, in the age of the perm, wore very long straight hair, sandals and not much make up. And there was a loud babble of foreign tongues. It all felt, well, continental.'[21]

Thring was disappointed that the number of subscribers was insufficient to maintain the theatre and that 'People have shown clearly they do not want the type of "theatre" we and others have tried to give them. They want superficial nonsense.'[22] Burke doesn't appear to have sought out further commissions for set design, although she later designed and printed the dramatic stage curtain design for the Canberra Civic Centre Theatre in 1965.

Guests in evening dress at the opening of the Arrow Theatre and its premier performance posed against curtains in Burke's *Tiger Stripe* design in November 1951.

Pages of a program for a season of *Othello* at the Arrow Theatre, featuring a Burke advertisement and a portrait of dashing young impresario, Frank Thring.

The finished set for *Enduring as the Camphor Tree*, which was staged at the former St Chad's church hall in 1946, in an outdoor performance at an outer suburban park in Ferntree Gully and in regional centres.

Burke painting a prop for *Enduring as the Camphor Tree*, an Australian play presented by the Little Theatre in 1946.

Fabie Chamberlin and Burke in the United States in the late 1940s.

THE LYCEUM CLUB, MELBOURNE

Established in 1912, the women-only Lyceum Club provided a place for university-educated women to meet and enjoy 'thoughtful' intellectual stimulation, relaxation and the pursuit of lifelong learning in an apolitical, nonsectarian environment. By the 1950s this commitment included those who had distinguished themselves in various professions, including the arts and business. Membership was via a proposal or nomination requiring at least two seconders; it is highly likely that Casey would have nominated the flattered Burke, who had not attended university but by the early 1950s was a creative and financial success in design and business. Joining the Lyceum Club would have complemented and broadened Burke's milieu and her closer friendship group in the postwar years.

A number of special interest groups known as 'circles' were offered, encouraging learning through sharing of mutual interests with an active program of talks, illustrated lectures and discussions. By 1954 Burke was reported to be active in the Art Circle and the Art Advisory group. When Mary Cecil Allen died in 1962 the Art Advisory group organised a memorial exhibition of her work with Casey, Burke and art educator Frances Derham all speaking at the opening. Curiously, Burke had no recorded involvement with the furnishings for the Lyceum Club's new premises, which opened in 1959; although a modern design, the conservative furnishing scheme was devised by Joyce Godfrey, an interior decorator who was also club president.

A watercolour drawing by club member and project architect Ellison Harvie, a partner of Stephenson & Turner, of the club building, which opened in 1959.

TRAVEL, INTERVIEWS AND WRITING

As soon as it was possible for her to travel overseas by air after the war, Burke flew to the United States and Canada, the first of a series of annual trips for the years 1947–50. Armed with letters of introduction from her friend Richard Casey, then a minister in the Commonwealth Government, Burke explored developments in design and retail, reporting to him on her return. Due to her travel and her experience in running successful design businesses, Burke was invited to be a founding member of the peak organisation for industrial design the Society of Designers for Industry (SDI), and was recognised as a prominent Australian 'tastemaker' and a frequently quoted expert on design and the home.

During her first trip Burke visited Hawaii and Toronto to view the cities' collections of Indigenous and Chinese art. She then travelled to New York, where she caught up with Allen, to Los Angeles and to San Francisco, which was known for its innovative department stores. On her return in September 1947 Burke was interviewed for an article syndicated to newspapers around Australia. It reported that she was impressed by the style of outdoor living she encountered and suggested it should be introduced in Australia. She also described as 'incredible' the labour-saving devices American housewives had at their disposal: 'The American housewife is not frightened of comfort … Comfort to her, is something she needs. She takes the view that she is not going to spend her life at the washtub.'[23] At this time few Australian homes had either washing machines or refrigerators; on washing day most women made use of coppers to boil whites and scrubbed clothes by hand. The interview also noted Burke's plans to commission local manufacturers to produce small labour-saving devices for the Australian housewife.

A month later Burke gave a lecture to the Housewives Association in Melbourne, organised through the SDI. She asserted that United States industrialists were more aware of the need 'to secure the opinion of women before going ahead to manufacture goods,'[24] in contrast to Australia, where she believed they were not consulted. Burke's argument about the lack of responsiveness to women consumers was frequently reported in the following year as she launched her retail business New Design, where she sold homewares and furniture both locally made and imported from the United States alongside her own fabrics. While it was true that Australian manufacturers lacked sophisticated research and marketing strategies at this time, Burke's comments cleverly implied that unlike other retailers, New Design offered goods chosen specifically for women's needs. Announcing that 'the time has come to be refreshed' and that she was focused on learning about developments in industrial design,[25] Burke took her second trip to the United States—this time taking in San Francisco, Atlanta and New Orleans—and her first to London and Paris in 1948. On her return, Burke declared

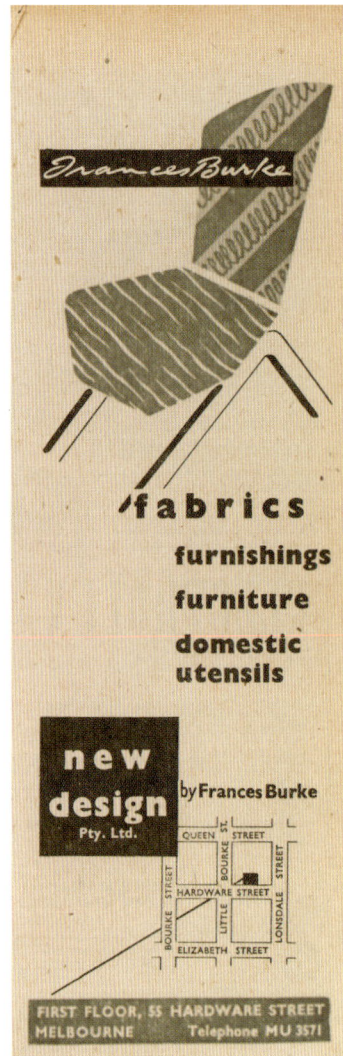

This graphic for Burke's retail business indicated that her designs could be used for upholstery in addition to curtains.

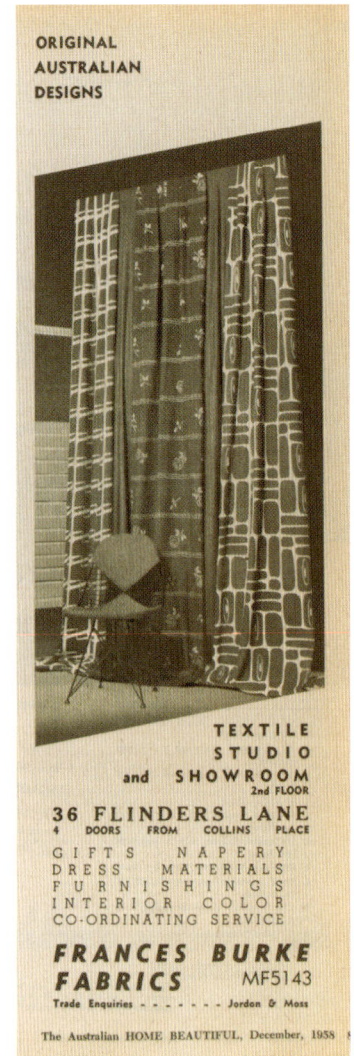

A Frances Burke Fabrics advertisement, including an Eames chair, attracting prospective clients to her studio and showroom. The chair, with 'bikini' pad, was manufactured in Sydney by Descon.

An advertisement for New Design with the vibrant colour that was central Burke's brand.

Burke in Milan, most probably taken by a street photographer, in front of the Duomo di Milano.
There is a handwritten message to Fabie Chamberlin on the reverse.

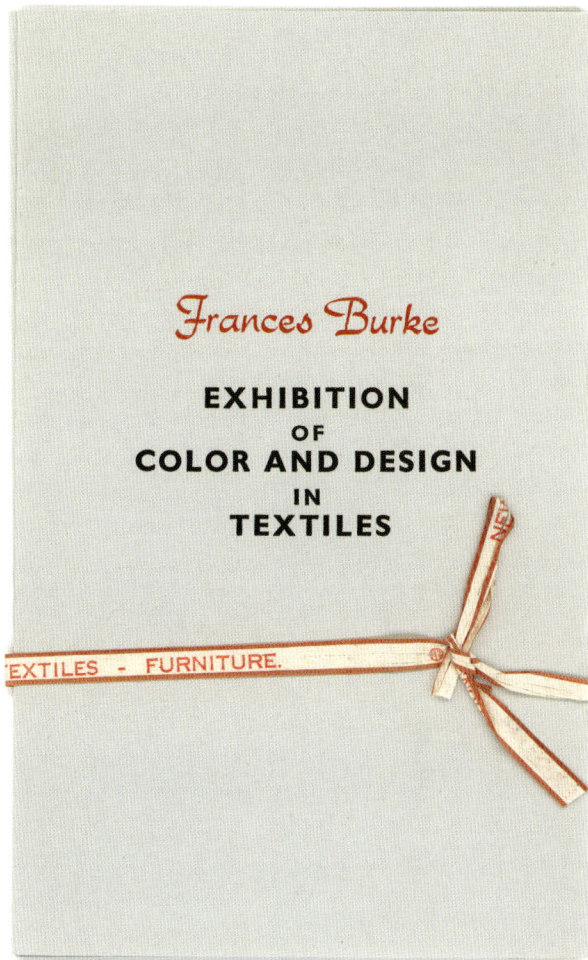

While the paper ribbon may not have been part of the original presentation of this booklet, Burke would have used it as discreet branding along with the characteristic plain brown paper in packaging her products.

that she was 'depressed by the unnecessary burden added to the cost of living in Australia by the lack of production'.[26]

The slow transformation of Australian industry from producing for the war to producing consumer goods was a result of the Commonwealth Government's choice to keep interest rates low in order to pay off the nation's war debt. Still unimpressed in 1951 by the gap in attitudes between the United States and Australia, Burke argued that 'Australian husbands and tradespeople—regard[ed] the housewife as a drudge'.[27] She insisted that homes needed more labour-saving devices, that there should be more deliveries of goods and a 'wider education in home-planning' to make domestic chores easier and less time-consuming. Unusually forthright for the time, Burke suggested that the remedy for this life of drudgery was in women's own hands—until 'Australian women break down this tradition they'll be expected to take their places quietly in the kitchen'.[28]

The selection of colours for interiors had long been accepted as a woman's domain. By the late 1940s Burke had begun disseminating her own ideas about colour for interiors on the basis of their psychological effect. She wrote and spoke about giving consideration to the function and aspect of a room; for example, using cool colours for hotter west-facing rooms and the application of colour in industrial settings to improve the safety of workers.[29] At a talk given to the Australian American Association, Burke commented on the way American designers used colour for a range of purposes and advocated 'greater use of colour in the design of public buildings, schools and hotel rooms'.[30] The widely syndicated article described her as a 'leading interior designer'. Burke argued it was time Australians began using bolder colours in their homes, and that Australia's strong light made the use of brighter colours not only possible, but essential. Seeking to position herself as a colour consultant to retail clients and to industry, Burke also described herself as both a 'textile designer and colourist'.[31]

An irresistible invitation to meet the designer and visit Burke's new studio.

Interviewed on her return from five months travelling in the United States, the United Kingdom, France and Italy in 1953, Burke reported on the increasing popularity of metal furniture. This comment was an implicit championing of local designer Clement Meadmore, who was also exploring the potential of steel furniture for the domestic market. She noted the increased simplification of fabric design and 'the more restrained and knowledgeable use of color in interior design'.[32] The 'great strides' that Burke perceived had been made in contemporary British furnishings since her previous visit to London were possibly due to the impact on popular taste of the 1951 Festival of Britain.

Although full of admiration for English design, Burke's greatest praise was for the ideas in the work of Italian designers. She was also impressed by the highly influential 'Good Design' collaboration between the Merchandise Mart Chicago and New York's Museum of Modern Art, whereby products that were selected as functional, well designed and manufactured were tagged with a 'Good Design' logo and promoted as such. The Merchandise Mart, twenty-five storeys high and two Chicago city blocks in length, was the largest building in the world when it opened in 1930. By 1953 trade shows presenting wholesalers' showrooms and convention spaces for real-time and televised events, attracted national and international retailers. Notes Burke made on her return in 1953 recorded that 'better goods are getting a better market this way & many of the stores are establishing their own Good Design sections. Very good for good design!' finishing with 'I wish we could do the same here!'[33]

In an article published in November 1954 for *Architecture and Arts*—a respected publication aimed at architects and the design cognoscenti that illustrates the measure of her influence—Burke was insistent that simple patterns and a limited number of colours were important in creating furnishing fabrics that harmonised with all the other design elements of an interior. She explained that soft furnishings 'are a highly satisfactory media for coordinating existing patterns in floor coverings and furniture' and that they 'can accent architectural style and define the character and functions of a room'.[34] Her arguments conveyed her understanding of furnishing fabrics as being most effective where they were subservient to the overall scheme rather than demanding attention as the dominant feature.

By 1956 Burke was at the peak of her career as a designer and was eagerly sought after as a commentator on modern design and colour in the home. As a result, she was commissioned to write a series of five articles titled 'Interior Design' for the *Weekly Times*. The topics to be covered were the practical aspects of using colour, light, lighting and space in home decoration. Burke used the opportunity provided by writing these articles to disseminate her ideas about good functional design, and to promote the work of local designers and her business. An article for *New Country Crafts* allowed Burke to give detailed advice about using pattern 'in a textural sense', by which she meant balancing plain and patterns across an interior, also explaining that a patterned curtain should have less fullness than a plain one. In her closing comments she argued, 'Original colour is just as much design as pattern.'[35]

This series of articles by and about Burke demonstrate her success in building her personal brand as an admired tastemaker and an effective communicator. Her early comments about the need for products to make women's lives easier, for improved services and for manufacturers to pay greater attention to the genuine needs of women were succeeded by advice on how to make effective choices in the elements of an interior. Together the articles show how her design philosophy was based on modernist ideas of functionalism and an embrace of progress, an understanding that technology could improve life, a belief that each element or unit including fabrics should contribute to an interior as a total design, and finally that in such interiors where simplicity reigned and colours were used effectively, design could provide a sense of well-being.

Another prestigious magazine cover: *Australian Home Beautiful* showing *Surf* in teal and *Squares* in red and gold colourways as inspiration for the homemaker.

Home Beautiful

AUSTRALIA'S HOW-TO-DO-IT MAGAZINE

OCTOBER, 1955 2/-

Registered in Australia for transmission by post as a periodical.

SPRING CURTAINS ISSUE

MAKE THIS DOLL'S HOUSE   pages 64, 66

An illustration for an article offering furnishing advice and a range of 'correct' designs, including *Band and Loop* and a grid design.[36]

The *Band and Loop* design (c. 1949).

A proof showing one of Burke's design methods—in this case the grid structure was printed onto paper. Seeing the printed form enabled the development of ideas for the balance and flow of the design units.

THE UNIT COLOUR DESIGNS

After twenty years designing and marketing textiles that were easily recognised and popular, in 1958 Burke selected a group to present to market under the brand 'Unit Colour Designs'. The creation of this new brand would have appealed to her as sound strategy, re-positioning and at the same time differentiating her already distinctive design range from competitors.

> Among Australian fabric designers and printers the name of Frances Burke has been the longest established … her fabrics have been used in many hotels, hospitals, clubs and other architect-designed buildings of note. However, equipment and technique have prevented her printing wider than 36in … As of this month, Frances Burke will begin Australia wide distribution of a few 'design favourites', printed on 48in cloth for her by a better equipped manufacturer. Price will be less than £1 per yard. Each to be known as a 'Unit Colour Design.'[37]

Burke often spoke and wrote of curtaining as forming a 'unit' of colour and texture in a space, so she would have understood the term 'unit' as an underlying concept in her design process, as textile design is fundamentally a series of units that are standardised then repeated, then applied to screens. One example of this process is her *Band and Loop* design, where variations were intermixed to yield different design outcomes.

The twenty Unit Colour Designs were offered to customers with the promise of speedier delivery and a reduced price for wider fabric. While initially it was only a limited range, all the designs had the appeal of being 'bestsellers'. According to her friend Anne Purves, Burke was a 'very practical, capable woman. Business and design are not incompatible and she found they were her talents.'[38] The Unit Colour Design range was Burke's solution to refreshing her brand after twenty years in business, enabling her to continue for another decade.

Marine designs

Marine motifs were among Burke's earliest fabric designs, commissioned for casual clothing and accessories; sun hats and bags, shorts, 'playsuits', bathing suits and 'beach coats', worn at the beach, river and lakeside. Just as the inventive depiction of plants had informed her floral designs, Burke continued exploring the potential of the marine environment to develop varied designs.

Many of Burke's marine designs incorporated a strong horizontal emphasis. *Starfish* (1938), one of her earliest designs, featured bands of five horizontal undulating lines suggesting the current, encircled by clusters of starfish. Larger in the foreground receding to smaller in the background, each starfish was depicted adrift and arms akimbo, apparently floating below the surface of the waves. This design was used to advantage as a furnishing fabric into the mid-1950s. Like *Starfish*, *Sea Horse* (1937) suggested creatures floating under the sea, but unusually for Burke it had two strongly contrasting colours and was an all-over design with a diagonal rather than a horizontal emphasis.

Sea Bits (1937) featured a wide band of seashells, coral, starfish, angelfish, stingrays and sponges. It also combined lines punctuated by tiny starfish, but this time suggesting a succession of waves leaving their mark upon the beach. While in *Starfish* the creatures were depicted in motion, in *Sea Bits* varied forms of sea life were laid out as if resting on the sand where a wave left them. An overhead view was seen again in *Surf* (1950), the graphic simplicity making it useful in promotions for Burke's business.

In 1946 Burke purchased land in Anglesea, on the coast south-west of Melbourne, subsequently building a tiny house in order to spend holidays at the beach. She loved observing the natural environment, collecting seashells to draw, painting landscapes and planting a native garden to blend in with the surrounding bush. *Crete* (1946), a design of the same year, marked a further shift in Burke's approach to a marine theme in placing alternating rows of highly stylised seashell and starfish motifs within a strong grid pattern, the scale of the motifs suggesting it was conceived as a furnishing fabric. Like the *Sea Bits* design, *Crete* was in negative, the contrasting curving and straight lines were formed by the white of base fabric while the printed colour filled in the background. The starfish motif was outlined by curling lines that suggested water lapping around its contours, while the shell's spiral form was suggested by two swirling arabesques converging towards its centre. When *Crete* was displayed in the window of Burke's Richmond showroom in the 1960s, she was delighted by a visit from an immigrant tradesman who tearfully praised the design, exclaiming that it vividly recalled traditional motifs throughout his family home on Crete.

Starfish (1938)

Sea Horse (1937)

Sea Bits (1937)

Surf (1950)

Crete (1946)

5

ARCHITECTURAL COLLABORATIONS AND COMMISSIONS

ARCHITECTURE

THE JOURNAL
OF THE ROYAL AUSTRALIAN
INSTITUTE OF ARCHITECTS

SPECIAL FEATURE
**ARCHITECTURE
OF ADVERTISING**

"HOUSE OF TOMORROW."
See page 22.

JANUARY, 1950

Registered at the G.P.O.,
Sydney, for transmission by
post as a periodical.

For the 1949 Modern Home Exhibition, Robin Boyd, designer of the House of Tomorrow, aimed to sweep away the past by presenting an entirely new approach to home design. With cantilevered box forms containing open-plan spaces, glass walls and individual feature walls painted in strong colours, the house polarised public opinion. Frances Burke's designs and plain dyed fabrics were chosen by Boyd to furnish the interiors.

n 1938, within a year of establishing her business, Frances Burke undertook a commission with a significant architectural practice, the first of many over the following three decades. The commissioned designs were her creative response to particular interiors and locations—from a luxury, tropical island resort to smart, sophisticated central city businesses. Architects recognised her parallel abilities: the subtle simplicity of her creative concepts that complemented their designs and her efficient and business-minded approach to project consultation. In turn, Burke admired architects and enjoyed working with them to create strikingly modern interiors.

Robin Boyd, leading Australian architect, theorist and writer, described an early interaction with Burke in *Lines*, the annual journal of the Architecture Students' Society of the Royal Victorian Institute of Architects (RVIA):

> One night Miss Burke packed a swatch of vivid samples and addressed the Architectural Students Society on the subject of fabric design, its aesthetic and technical aspects. The nature of the process permits … fabrics custom-printed for exclusive and particular jobs. Architects and interior decorators know and use these materials, and are grateful for them.[1]

Burke's talk for architectural students on textile design and the role it played in interior design was a sound business strategy and almost certainly resulted in commissions.

In addition to her talk for architecture students, this arresting double-page spread in *Lines* gave Burke significant profile among young architects.

The Arists Embark

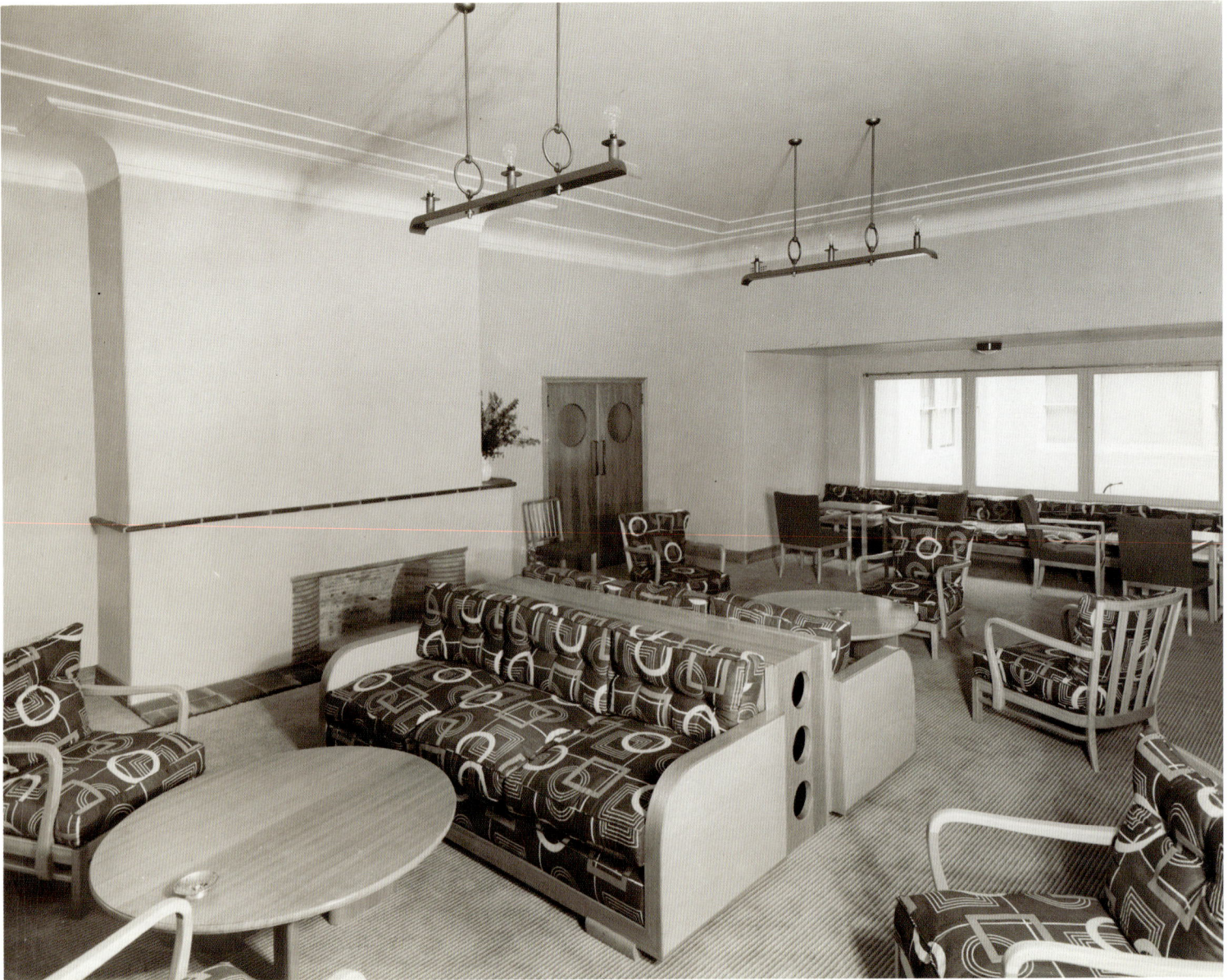

The lounge of Erskine House by Buchan, Laird & Buchan, Lorne (1938–39).

This early design stands out as being unusually complex—the tightly fitting shapes in three colours would require intricate registration. The motifs Burke used responded to those of the lounge interior.

BUCHAN, LAIRD & BUCHAN: ERSKINE HOUSE

The first of Burke's architectural collaborations was with the progressive Geelong practice Buchan, Laird & Buchan, who in the 1930s had begun to 'shape the architectural language of Geelong' with a range of modern buildings.[2] Burke produced furnishings for their extension to Erskine House, a seaside guesthouse established in 1888 in Lorne, on the south-west coast of Victoria, where many affluent Western District, Geelong and Melbourne families holidayed, often during the same weeks each summer.

Burke's design for the Erskine House lounge room responded effectively to the geometry of the architecture, furniture and lighting. A newspaper journalist commended 'the cheerful gay effects necessary for a bright holiday guest house',[3] while the RVIA Students' Society monthly news-sheet *Smudges* asserted that 'it is the interiors that really win these plaudits', praising 'the architect designed furniture, and the selection of fabrics, especially the dark blue Burway linens in the lounge'.[4] This project brought acclaim and opened a new direction for Burke's fledgling business towards furnishings and away from fashion.

Smudges was artfully planned in terms of layout, then carefully folded for mailing purposes. Editor Robin Boyd awarded the recently opened Erskine House the 'Bouquet of the Month', as opposed to the 'Blot of the Month'.

THE STUDENTS SOCIETY OF THE ROYAL VICTORIAN INSTITUTE OF ARCHITECTS.

SMUDGES

A News Sheet for the Profession.

R. PENLEIGH BOYD, Editor, 4 Bank Place.
C. MERVYN MORGAN, Managing Editor.

No. 1   Associates:
Vol. 2   R. McC. SIMPSON.
Jan., 1940.   P. E. NEWELL.

EDITORIAL

SALUTATIONS OF 1940

The mockery of peace and goodwill at Christmas gives way to complete antithesis of a Happy New Year.

Presaged by the roll of guns and heralded by the glare of world-wide conflagration, 1940 has made its grim entry. What will it bring, this year of trepidation and uncertainty?

Who can say? It may be a year of intense and prosperous activity. City building work is maintaining its busy level; many large jobs are on the board and are about to commence. Industrial work is bound to increase in proportion to our supply quota for the International demands.

Uncertainty and more uncertainty "Smudges" is desolated at being unable to send you assurance, and wish you prosperity. It does nevertheless propagate the firm hope that as Architects and Architectural students we shall be given the opportunity to dedicate our skill towards the preservation of a rational civilisation.

.. THE JANUARY REVIEW ..

PRETTY PUBS

Australians have always been famed for their partiality to beer, but, judging from the progress our hotel designers are making, we will never become famous for the surroundings in which we drink it.

Recently there has been great activity in hotel building, and remodelling—many blots and one bouquet—but the pubs of yore have yielded to an onslaught of crude modernity. Formerly the pub, in deference to our outworn tradition, was cast in the Elizabethan inn design—an ideal place for escapists to further forget in their cups the cruel world outside.

Now the low beamed bar and garish leadlights are replaced by the inevitable tiles, strip lettering and poorly designed, good, honest glass, sandblasted out of recognition. Occasionally, there is a throw back to the Tudor tavern—as that practical joke on the new Hoddle Bridge testifies.

But hotel design, if anything, has become even duller and more monotonous.

Let us look to England and see that mockery and vulgarity have been discarded, and that pleasant, airy hotels, are beginning to appear on the landscape. The new Hotel Australia and Erskine House have given a splendid example of what the residential hotel can be.

We strive to attract tourists to our shores, and they expect at least the standards they are used to at home; that's not asking much.

Boquet of the Month

To architects Buchan, Laird and Buchan, for Erskine House, Lorne.

BLOT OF THE MONTH

ORRONG HOTEL, Orrong Road and High Street corner, Armadale.
For High Street—a vulgar heap.

FRANKSTON HOTELS

The rival remodellings of two of Frankston's hotels has resulted in one orthodox solution—The Pier Hotel—and one which steps just a little out of the groove. The Grand Hotel has decidedly queer proportions, and some even queerer details, but it does invite.

The two-storey pub is indeed a problem. Unsatisfactory solutions crowd the corners of every Australian town (refer Blot of this month and of last November). If Frankston's Grand Hotel is not an outstanding example of contemporary architecture, it at least has struck a happy and seldom achieved medium between uninviting dullness and repellent vulgarity.

.. GUEST HOUSE :

ERSKINE HOUSE, LORNE

The singular and exciting opportunities of Guest House design are all too frequently overlooked in this country. We should be, in fact are, notorious for the primitiveness of our country and seaside hotelries. Of these, the latter is the more insidious type. And for the countless classes of guest house and hotel, good, ordinary and bloody, you will find a fair average specimen in "lovely" Lorne.

At last Lorne has approached architectural justification of the magnificent environment nature has given it. Erskine House extensions, recently completed by Buchan, Laird & Buchan, provide a brilliant relief from the usual gay, bizarre, beach and sand atmosphere.

Externally the building is simply treated with white painted brickwork, matching existing additions completed two summers since. Good plain white walls rise three floors to the rust coloured pitched roof. The well-proportioned and pleasantly varied fenestration shows an intelligent appreciation of the case.

But it is the interiors which really win these plaudits. We like: The quarry tile paving to the entrance hall; the well proportioned lounge rooms with their subtle colour schemes—all different, yet all combining in harmonious totality; the architect-designed furniture, and the selection of fabrics, especially the dark blue Burway linens in the lounge; the fine canvas hanging to the stair hall window; the anodised metal light fittings (except for the pop shop 3 ball motif used in the smoke room), and the buckram drum like shades to the dining room lights.

Here in fact is a successful and delightful job. By no means free of the influence of moderne banformen it shows a usually intelligent appreciation of recent Continental work occasionally adapted to enhance our local materials and countryside.

AND HOTEL ARCHITECTURE :

HANS PETER OSER: HELENA RUBINSTEIN SALON

A subsequent and very different commission came from Viennese émigré architect Hans Peter Oser, who in 1940 commissioned Burke to produce curtains for the salon of international cosmetics entrepreneur Helena Rubinstein, in the St James Building, Castlereagh Street, Sydney. Oser's training at Vienna Technical University, his experience working under Josef Hoffmann and Peter Behrens, and his European sophistication were perfect for Rubinstein's sumptuous new salon.[5]

Oser configured the space to provide a reception room, make-up bar and treatment rooms. In the reception room, full-length wall mirrors alternated with luxurious fabric panels including a handblocked print on silk described by leading Sydney interior decorator Molly Grey as 'a tiger lily motif … in pale coral and turquoise on an ivory ground'.[6] An afternoon cocktail party celebrating the salon's opening drew a mix of high society and cultural figures, including prima ballerina Tamara Toumanova and dancer-choreographer Nina Verchinina from the Ballets Russes.[7] The contrast between provincial seaside guesthouse and glamorous central Sydney salon speaks of Burke's agility in designing for diverse environments.

Tiger Lily (c. 1940)

The north-facing site inspired Grounds' development of the Quamby flats, though it appeared dry, rocky and inhospitable, particularly compared with the luxuriant gardens in other parts of Toorak.

ROY GROUNDS: QUAMBY

In the same year, ambitious architect Roy Grounds commissioned Burke to work on his remarkable development Quamby, a block of six flats in Glover Court, Toorak—a smart Melbourne address. Architecturally significant and influential, Quamby was skilfully designed to respond to a difficult site—a rocky outcrop left undeveloped for many years, featuring extensive views to the north over the Yarra River to the city. 'In Quamby, what had previously been mere architectural boxes were now treated with imagination and were fanned out towards a view.'[8] This development offered an informal way of life with well-detailed kitchens, and living and dining areas flooded with light from their large north-facing windows.

Rangga was designed for this 'very modern block of flats'; Burke recalled that 'no-one had ever heard of a kitchen in a living room unless it was in the slums, they hadn't thought of it ever being in ... beautifully built flats in Toorak.'[9] The pale walls and light-coloured wood fittings meant that the fabric, featuring strong graphic Aboriginal-inspired motifs, enhanced the space through its scale without overwhelming it. The choice of colours skilfully linked the interior with the native grasses and tawny sandstone rocks of the immediate landscape.[10] Quamby consolidated Grounds' reputation as an important twentieth-century Australian architect, and together with two other blocks of flats, Moonbria and Clendon, had a dramatic influence on postwar flat design in Melbourne.

One of the six sophisticated, sun-filled flats in the Quamby development; the kitchen, although deftly hidden, was 'revolutionary' in occupying part of the living space.

This flat, showing a restrained colour scheme incorporating Burke's
Rangga fabric, was the one Roy Grounds retained for his own use.

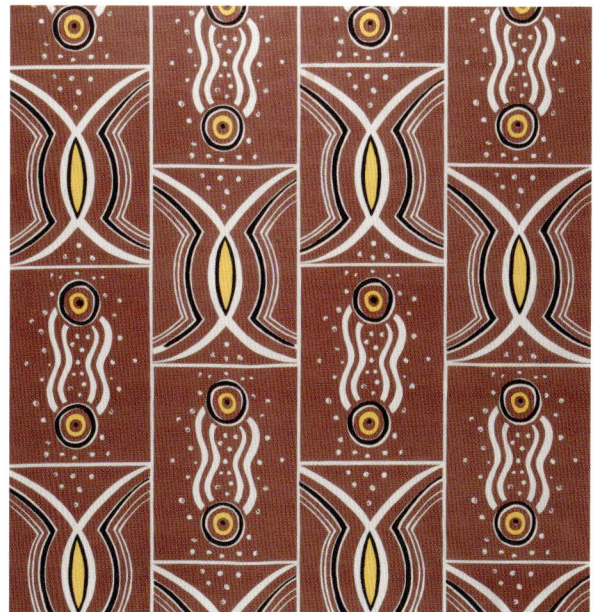

Rangga (1940)

GUILFORD BELL: ANSETT HAYMAN ISLAND RESORT

Ansett became a household name in Australia, one which was synonymous with domestic travel in the postwar period. In 1947 the transport magnate and far-sighted aviation pioneer Reginald Ansett purchased Hayman Island in the Whitsunday archipelago off the Queensland Coast, aiming to extend Ansett Airlines' services by transforming the island into Australia's most fashionable beach resort. Hayman Island offered a unique opportunity to create unprecedented luxury in a lush setting, accessed in the most exciting and romantic way—by seaplane. Genevieve Lansell, the niece of Zara Holt, recalled:

Hayman Island was frightfully smart, I went with Reg by flying boat from Rose Bay in Sydney, via Lord Howe Island, when I was working for Ansett on the overseas desk and then when Cyril and I married we went for our honeymoon … Manyung Hotel and Reg Ansett's house were full of Frances' fabrics too.[11]

The architects Guilford Bell, who had studied architecture in London, and John La Gerche, with whom Bell had served in the Australian Air Force during World War II, produced a detailed site plan. Appointed site manager for the duration of the project until its completion in 1952, Bell controlled 'ferries, dredges, a small railway, a sawmill and workshops, and oversaw up to 500 workers'.[12] 'All building materials had to come from the mainland by barge, and during construction Guilford was virtually king of the island'. Bell certainly made his mark on Hayman Island—everything 'was created and designed by Guilford, including the gardens—he had a nursery on the island and propagated plants for landscaping'.[13]

Burke, whose work Bell would have known through his friendship with Roy Grounds, was commissioned to design and produce furnishing textiles. Collecting a range of objects from a Hayman beach, Bell sent them to Burke in Melbourne for inspiration. She lamented that 'people later said to me you must have had a lovely time going up and down to Hayman Island but … I never walked past my own studio … The plans told me the size of the rooms, the function of the room … and finally we evolved half a dozen … designs'.[14]

Gordon Shebly, one of Burke's screen printers, recorded in his diary in early March 1949: 'Very hot today … proofed new Ansett design fish [sic], looks great'. A few weeks later,

Facing the beach, the cabins at Hayman Island offered a level of privacy, which was one factor that led to it becoming a highly successful honeymoon destination.

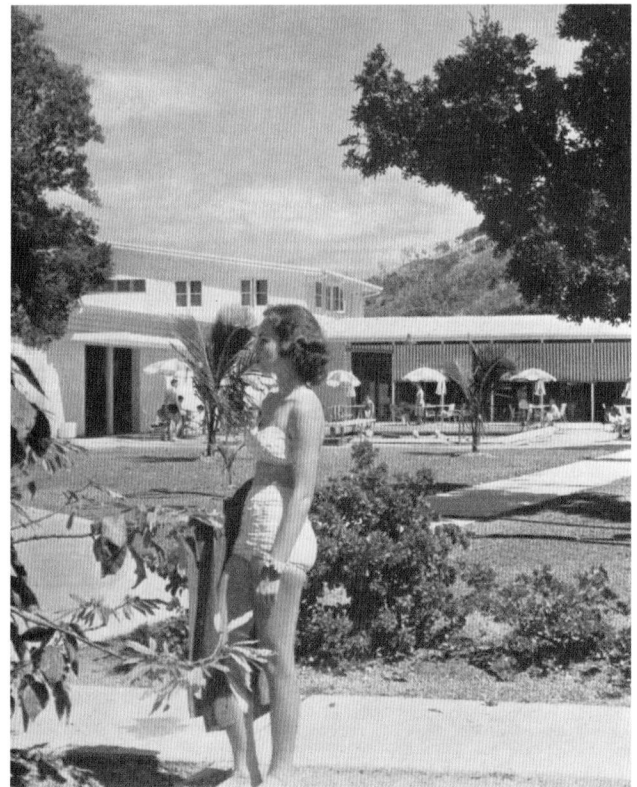

The guests experienced lush tropical plants, grown on the island in Bell's nursery, in the open areas and on the walk between the beachside cabins, bar and dining room.

This cabin interior shows Burke's *Angel Fish* fabric setting the mood—relaxation island style: a read on the bed and only a short step across the sand for a swim.

Angel Fish (1949)

Designed to cover an entire wall of the public space of the resort, the sophisticated
Seapiece shows Burke's masterly ability to juxtapose positive and negative shapes.

he wrote: 'I printed new design today *Tropical*, very nice', and subsequently, 'we started on the Ansett order today, going to be a job, with new designs and colours'. Shebly's final mention of the work for Ansett was on 4 December: 'Hot day, up to 92 [degrees Fahrenheit] I printed *Sea Star* all day finished the Ansett order'.[15]

When it opened in 1950 the Royal Hayman Island Hotel consisted of a large central dining room, bar and lounge areas with an entertainment stage.

> The complex captured the glamour of international tourism … As a type, Hayman Island was the first post-war purpose-built tourist resort in Australia. The sort of clientele who flew to the Barrier Reef in the early 1950s were rich, mobile and cosmopolitan. Many guests were impressed with the stylish ease of the resort and its entirely co-ordinated combination of landscape and architectural design. For others, it was their first experience of post-war modern architecture.[16]

The Hayman Island project created a profile for Guilford Bell and exposure to an affluent clientele that enabled him to set up in a successful private practice in Melbourne in 1952. In responding to Bell's collection of shells, sponges and other sea life, Burke developed a set of clever, fresh, contemporary designs that successfully embedded her as a significant figure in the development of an Australian modernism. Since Ansett didn't negotiate exclusivity, Burke continued selling the designs over the following decades—specifically *Seapiece*, *Angel Fish* and *Sea Star*. This project led to further commissions for Burke, including providing fabric for accommodation at a ski resort in the New South Wales town of Cooma, the Southern Cross Ski Club lodge at Mount Buller, Victoria, and hotels in central and northern Australia.

Southern Cross fabric, in blue, as used in the Mount Buller ski lodge.

Burke's *Southern Cross* fabric shown in situ in the wood-panelled Southern Cross ski lodge at Mount Buller (c.1950), with club president Peter Goodman in the foreground.

Burke's *Wavy Stripe* made a subtle but modern divan bed cover in the Robin Boyd–designed House of Tomorrow.

ROBIN BOYD: THE 1949 MODERN HOME EXHIBITION

In recognition of Burke's growing profile as a designer of furnishing textiles, her work featured prominently in an exhibition of modern architecture and design that resonated well beyond the city of Melbourne. The 1949 Modern Home Exhibition held in the Royal Exhibition Building and themed 'Yesterday, Today and Tomorrow' aimed to showcase modern architectural solutions and good functional design.

Robin Boyd designed the small (100 square metre) but arresting two-storey display home, the House of Tomorrow, which was constructed within the Exhibition Building and fitted out in ten days under the direction of Boyd's assistant, architecture student Peter McIntyre. Through the large, unglazed windows visitors could imagine themselves in a home with a modern, open floorplan within a modest footprint. The interiors incorporated the newest products designed by members of the Society of Designers for Industry. These included Grant Featherston's chairs, and low cupboards and tables in Australian native timbers; Burke's fabric *Wavy Stripe* used for a bed cover, *Moresque* for cushions in the living room and a Marine blue for the curtain in the kitchen–dining room; brightly coloured, innovative lighting units by BECO; paintings by Arthur Boyd and ceramics by Allan Lowe and Martin Boyd.

The daring, vibrant exterior colours of the house were variously described as 'mauve and marine' or purple and blue-green, while the interiors also had feature walls of contrasting colours and textures. McIntyre recalled the paint was supplied by local company Tip Top Paints (1940–56), which offered a range of contemporary colours appealing to the new generation of architects and homeowners. Commenting in *The Age*, Boyd described the House of Tomorrow as a 'gallery of modern Australian design in everyday things ... All of these items are available to any home builders ... None of them is in the luxury price group ... Here they have been collected for the first time in a combined display of modern Australian industrial art'.[17]

Tip Top Paints presented their colour range in the Coloramic flip manual to assist the undecided homeowner make a final decision on paint colour.

Providing an accent of strong colour, *Moresque* design was used as a cushion cover.

Wavy Stripe, 1948.

In 1951 Boyd designed the demonstration *Sunshine House* representing the *Age* RVIA Small Homes Service at the Exhibition Building as part of the Jubilee Better Homes and Housekeeping Exhibition. In his defense of its bold colours, Boyd wrote that they 'might look odd and even offensive to some people' but that they 'offend because they are strong and determined and express a point of view instead of a neutral, timid evasion'.

In the Melbourne *Herald*, design writer Edna Horton-Lewis advised the public that it was important to abandon their 'fears and prejudices' regarding modern design—it seems many did, as the attendance reached over 60 000 in two weeks.

For the Ideal Home Show in 1952 Boyd, with Bruce Anderson, a director of Andersons Furniture, coordinated the display of 'Bad Taste' and 'Good Taste' rooms, which were intended to contrast the best and worst of local design. The Good Taste room showcased curtains in Burke's *Oak Leaf* fabric, together with a Featherston Contour chair, a Meadmore lamp and a Snelling Line cabinet—a quietly stylish interior signalling the design mix of the decade.

The 'Bad Taste' room looks crowded and stuffy, whereas the 'Good Taste' room, despite its nod to English design heritage in the oak leaf motif used in the curtains, is a breath of fresh air.

Oak Leaf (1940)

PROJECTS FOR COMMUNITIES

Although Burke designed for the affluent—seen in her work on beach resorts in Lorne and Hayman Island, and in the supply of her fabrics to a range of residences in wealthy suburbs—she was also committed to projects that benefitted the broader public.

> I felt that if I became an artist … my work would only be known to a few—the wealthy—who could afford to buy pictures and were acquainted with European culture. But through textiles … my ideas would reach a greater number of people who might be influenced to better taste and whose values would be improved, their appreciation of the beautiful increased, and their enjoyment of life enriched.[18]

While the lofty aims of improving public taste and values through design and colour are an anachronism, Burke, having switched career from nursing to textile design in 1937, was well placed to have thought through some of the implications of colour and interior design for spaces devoted to public health. As a result, architects and others specifying interior fit-outs for hospitals, kindergartens, welfare centres and hostels ordered her fabrics: giving Burke an opportunity to contribute to the community's well-being in these spaces.

Hospitals

Burke supplied fabric in the postwar period to sixteen Australian hospitals; her fabrics were used 'for bedspreads, sofa covers, cushions, curtains, room dividers and bed screens … the buyers looked at the practical angle first and then found they loved the effects'.[20] Hospital projects enlivened by Burke's fabrics included the nurses' home at Prince Henry's Hospital, South Melbourne, designed in 1950 by architects Leighton Irwin; the midwifery wing at Bendigo Base Hospital, Victoria, in 1952, by Yuncken, Freeman Brothers & Simpson; the maternal wing at the Footscray and District Hospital in 1953, by Bates, Smart & McCutcheon; and the 1956–58 extension and refurbishment of the Freemason's Hospital in East Melbourne, by Meldrum & Noad, which was originally designed by Stephenson & Meldrum in 1937.

A large percentage of Burke's hospital commissions came from the practice of Stephenson & Turner, architects of 'the most internationally celebrated of Australia's buildings of the era'.[21] Burke's fabrics were supplied to a range of their projects, including the Royal Melbourne Hospital in 1941; the Alfred Hospital, Melbourne, in 1948; the Queen Elizabeth Hospital, Adelaide, in 1959; and the Royal Children's Hospital, Melbourne, in 1963. Arthur Stephenson was recognised as the 'world's leading specialist hospital architect and the firm as Australia's most prominent practice'.[22]

Burke proudly stated that she 'did a complete fit-out of Freemasons … from top to toe'.[19]

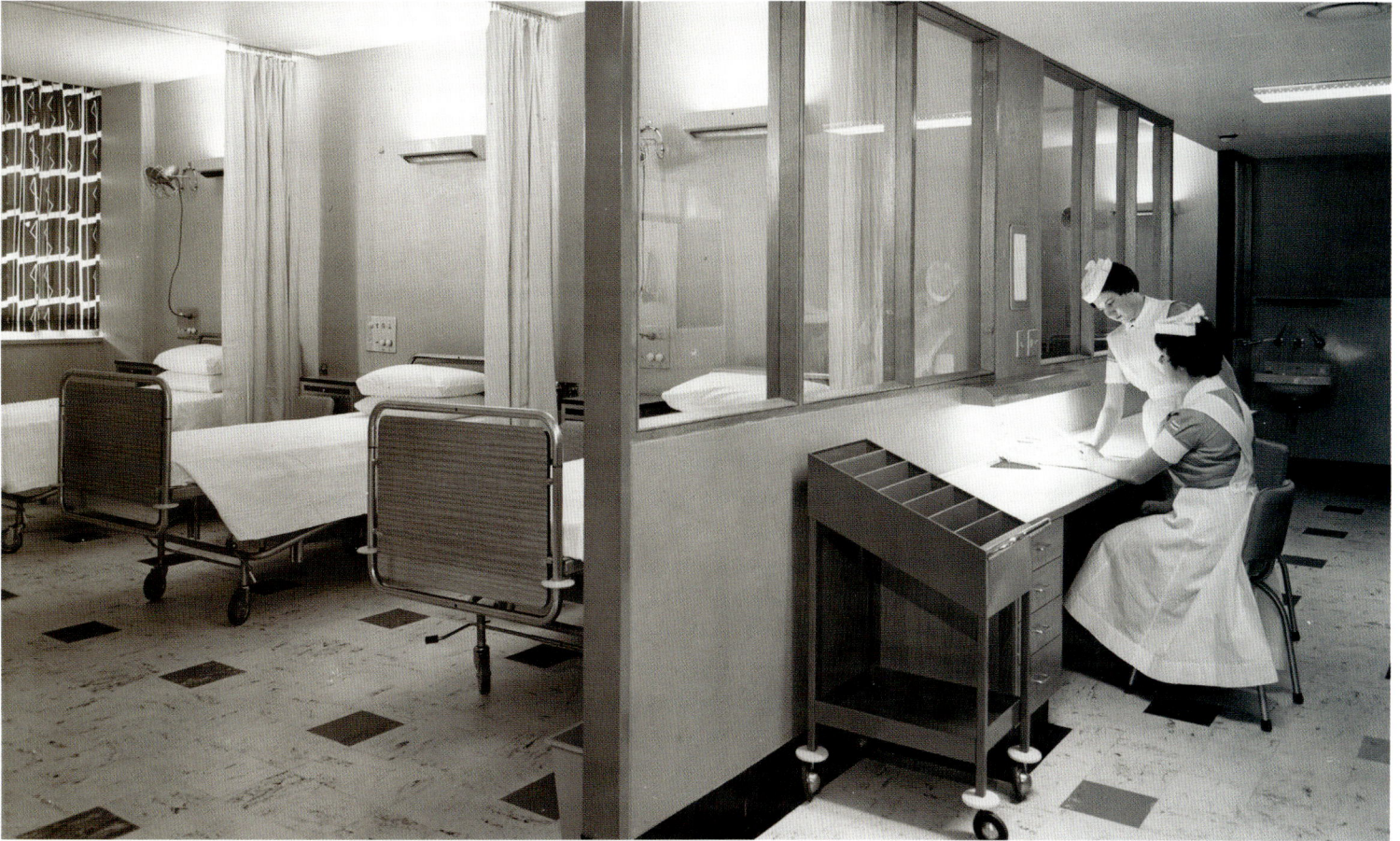

The energetic, upbeat *Pacifica* design featured in a ward of the new
Queen Elizabeth Hospital main block, Adelaide, South Australia, 1959.

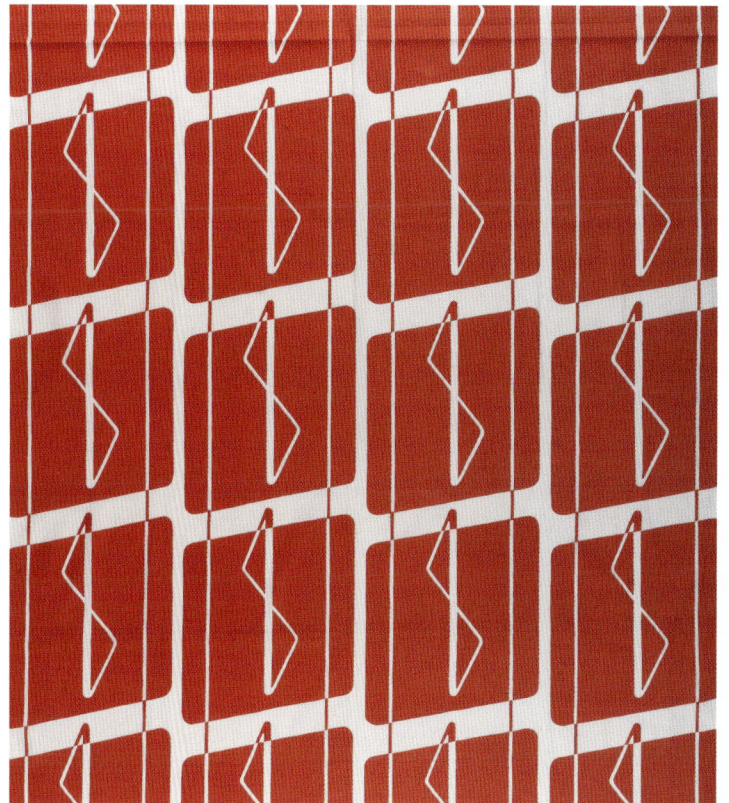

Pacifica (1953)

The flowing lines of *Canna Leaf* were chosen for curtains and chairs in the visitors'
lounge of the nurse's home at the Royal Melbourne Hospital (c. 1941).

A newborn baby in a humidicrib at The Alfred
Hospital, 1948. The *Koala* curtains were chosen to
make the space less intimidating and the parents
perhaps less fearful.

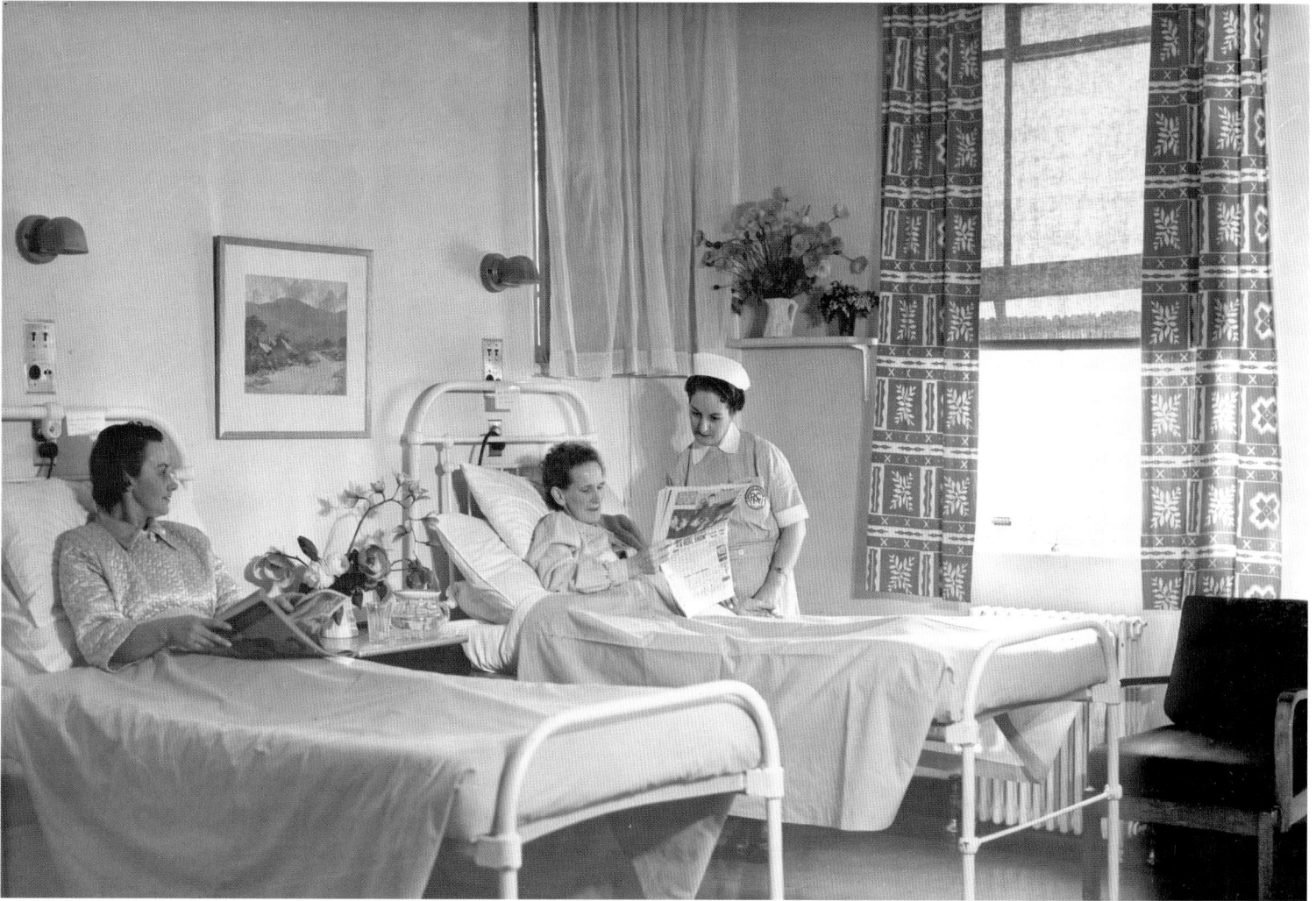

A ward in the Peter MacCallum Clinic, 1954, with *Moresque* curtains.

Stephenson's capacity to land the contracts and drive the design of large hospital projects was legendary. He understood the importance of marshalling all aspects of design in creating hospitals as healthy, positive places filled with fresh air and sunlight. Burke's talents were recognised by the practice, her designs contributing to its vision for modern hospitals. The practice was exceptional in employing and promoting women architects, including Mary (Mollie) Turner Shaw, who designed and supervised the fit-out of interiors, and the brilliant Ellison Harvie, who was promoted as lead architect and project manager on the largest of their sites, the Royal Melbourne Hospital in Parkville. Harvie would have signed off the fit-out of the hospital's ten-storey nurses' home, which was furnished 'with over 1,000 yards of different Frances Burke fabrics.'[23]

In addition to working with architects, Burke was also contacted directly by hospitals to work with them. Prior to the Victorian Hospitals Association's establishment of a central ordering system, representatives from each of the hospitals came to Burke's showroom to discuss their needs and make their selections.

Burke's 1951 refurbishment of the headquarters of the College of Nursing for the Australian United Nurses' Association and the Australian Nursing Federation was widely praised: 'Throughout the centre has been redecorated by Frances Burke who has used bold unusual colour schemes. These are designed to enhance the lovely proportions of the various rooms and bring an atmosphere of brightness and warmth into some and produce a feeling of restful quiet in others.'[24] This interior decoration commission led to an invitation in May 1951 for Burke to give a talk for nurses, which she titled 'Colour and Design in Everyday Life'. Another refurbishment, this time for the Peter MacCallum Clinic at Little Lonsdale Street, Melbourne, in 1954, included at least six of Burke's designs: *Crete*, *Staccato*, *Squares*, *Tiger Lily*, *Tiger Stripe* and *Moresque*.

Child health and welfare

Prior to World War II, kindergartens were conceived as providing a remedial experience for poor and otherwise disadvantaged children, but after the war, well-organised and 'profitably run preschool education came to be seen by many as the standard for all levels of Australian society'.[25] This was the result of efforts by early childhood educators, parents, philanthropists and the federal government to develop model centres in each state capital. The first of these model kindergartens, named Lady Gowrie Centres—admired by Robin Boyd as well planned, easily understood and lacking affectation—was completed in 1938.[26] Located in the inner Melbourne suburb of Carlton, it was designed by society architect Marcus Martin and became the template for future centres.

Inspired by the light, bright Lady Gowrie model, the Isabel Henderson Free Kindergarten was one of many that sprang up in the postwar period. It opened on Green Reserve in Alexandra Parade, Fitzroy, in March 1950, on ground made available by the Fitzroy Council.[27] It was named in honour of a pioneer of child welfare in Victoria, also the founder and first principal of Clyde Girls School. The Clyde Old Girls committee undertook to equip the Martin-designed kindergarten and to raise £250 per year towards its running costs. Two 'large airy nurseries' were painted in pink and blue, one 'with blue and white print curtains designed by Frances Burke … and the other with salmon pink and white curtains'.[28]

The postwar 'baby boom', which began in 1946 and peaked in 1951, together with a national commitment to child health and welfare, led to the construction of baby health centres throughout Australian suburbs and towns. Many followed the lead of hospitals and kindergartens in creating bright interiors using Burke's fabrics as a welcoming feature, softening the spaces and making them feel less institutional. The Canberra Mothercraft Society chose *The Hunt* for the curtains for their new city centre in 1948, combining the maternal and child welfare service with an occasional care centre for preschool children. At the Keppell Street, Carlton Baby Health Centre in 1951, contemporary furnishings included 'Danish cork tiled floors … walls … in soft pink and ceilings in pale blue or blue green. Curtains and chair covers are attractive cotton prints by textile designer Frances Burke'.[29]

Melbourne City Council Pre School medical officer Dr Bell Broderick examining a child in 1951, with curtains of Burke's design *Hispano* in the background.

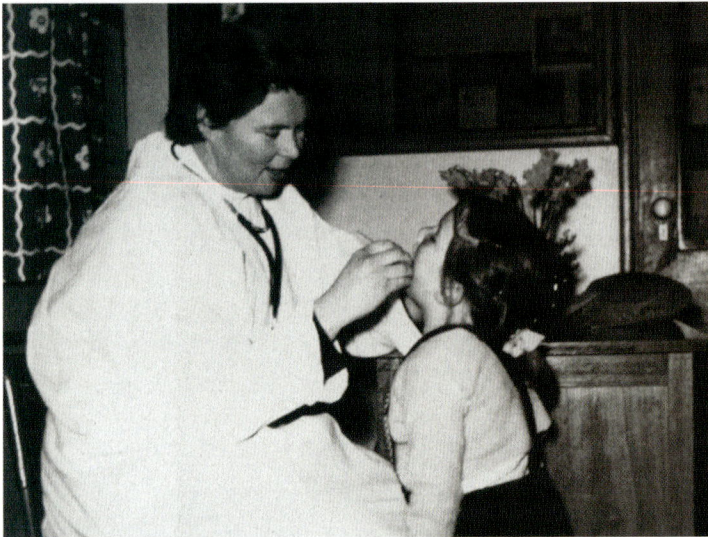

Hispano (1940)

Mothers and babies at the Canberra Mothercraft Society Centre
in front of the new curtains in *The Hunt* design.

Featuring Burke's *Tiger Stripe*, the Yallourn Baby
Health Centre opened in 1949 to cater for the
expanding community.

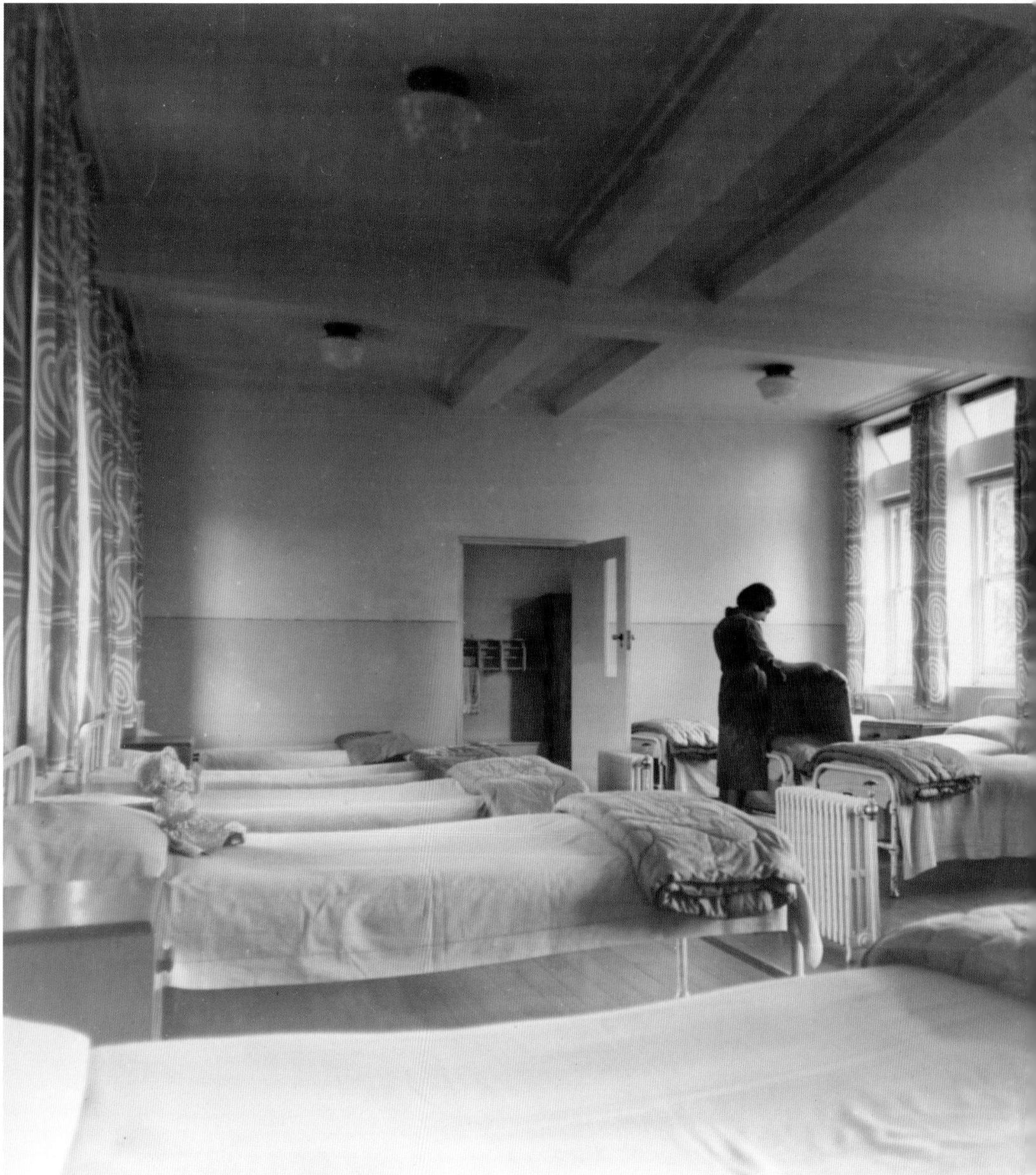

A dormitory at Travancore, where the Burke fabric *Willy* was used to create a softer, more homely feel.

Willy (1945)

By 1952 Burke's evolving interest in the effects of colour included its use as therapy, to which she referred after supplying fabrics and advice on paint colour to Travancore.[30] Opened in the early 1930s, the Melbourne residential school and clinic for children needing psychiatric treatment was 'surrounded by beautiful lawns, gardens and sports grounds … while a Toddlers' Block and playroom are for the smaller ones. Attached is a dormitory, a sick bay and fine sunrooms.'[31] Burke subscribed to the now discredited theory that colour contributed to the treatment of a range of conditions; today it is recognised that colour may have a positive effect on mood and in particular on a sense of well-being, rather than actually constituting treatment. At the least, 'Burke enlivened with bright walls and designs that she thought would interest the young.'[32]

Company towns

In the postwar years the State Electricity Commission of Victoria upgraded the workers' facilities in the model company town, Yallourn, Gippsland, where the brown coal open-cut mine linked with the new Morwell Power Station to generate electricity for Melbourne. Wooden huts that housed single workers of both genders were supplemented in 1948 by a substantial brick dwelling furnished with Burke's fabrics, a commission of which she was particularly proud. Burke continued forming her ideas regarding the use and effects of colour in interiors, and in this project gave considerable thought to creating warm and welcoming living spaces for the workers.

The Eildon Weir, north-east of Melbourne, was another major postwar infrastructure project—providing water storage for the city—requiring the construction of a township for workers. In addition to hostels and shops, entertainment was also provided: 'During the construction days, movies were shown every night and a talented revue company was formed from the local population. Variety shows and plays were performed frequently.'[33] The Eildon Theatre, supported by a grant of £100 from the Little Theatre for which Burke had designed stage sets in the 1940s, was delivered in 1951 by architects Bates, Smart & McCutcheon. The theatre interior was predominantly timber with some blue painted wall panels, wooden seating and a curtain in Burke's design *Willy*, which completed the scheme.

An aerial view of the Eildon township and the completed Eildon Weir.

A surprisingly sophisticated space, the Eildon Theatre featured a row of lights illuminating the stage curtains in Burke's *Willy* design (1951).

①

E

②

③

④

⑤

⑥

Dr Ernest Fooks looking dapper in his trademark
bow tie, photographed in his new office in
Woonsocket Court in St Kilda; also captured are
curtains in a version of *Shields* fabric.

Shields (c. 1953)

Offices

As early postwar restrictions on constructing commercial premises were lifted and business conditions improved in the 1950s, architects were presented with a range of new opportunities—to design factories, offices and shops. Some more entrepreneurial architects also acted as property developers: Austrian émigré architect Dr Ernest Fooks, for example, moved his practice to Woonsocket Court, St Kilda, in 1956, choosing Burke fabric to reflect the sophistication of this new development. It was one 'of the relatively few examples in Melbourne of a purpose-built architectural office, designed by and for a prominent post-war architect. This particular office, incorporating flats, was said to be the first example in Melbourne of this new type.'[34]

The American food company Kraft commissioned Oakley & Parkes & Partners to design and supervise the construction of a new factory complex at Port Melbourne to open in 1957. Designer Dudley V Peck & Associates of Collins Street,

Melbourne—a specialist in office planning—was in turn commissioned to design the interiors, and Burke's *Wavy Stripe* was selected for the factory's boardroom.

Architect Harry Ernest, winner of the 1952 Stephenson & Turner Gold Medal for Architecture as the outstanding fourth year student at the University of Melbourne, established his own practice in 1955. While undertaking residential work, Ernest also obtained commissions for commercial buildings, including Chelsea House at 55 Flemington Road, North Melbourne. It was the first building in Melbourne with glass and steel curtain walls on all four sides. Another of Ernest's later commercial commissions was for the new headquarters of Mono Pumps in Lower Dandenong Road, Mordialloc, Melbourne in 1965.[35] The modest-sized office building included a stylish boardroom, with a view to the garden courtyard framed by curtains in Burke's *Lunar* design.

Architects: Oakley & Parkes & Partners
Office Planning & Furniture.
Dudley V. Peck & Associates.
Photographs of the Kraft Foods Ltd.
Factory, Port Melbourne, by
Gordon F. De Liste.

FROM THE FOYER

TO THE MEETING ROOM

EFFICIENT
OFFICE PLANNING
for Industry and Commerce

DUDLEY V. PECK
& ASSOCIATES

111 Smith St., Fitzroy
JA 5338
•
41 Collins St., Melbourne

Do your Offices provide

Good Staff accommodation without waste of space?
Efficient work flow without undue movement of people or papers?
Good working conditions including lighting, colour, furniture, ventilation, noise factors and staff amenities?
Easily applied managerial and supervisory control?
A flexible layout with allowance for future expansion?

Ring, write or call for   full details *without* obligation.

Interior design consultant Dudley V Peck took a functionalist approach, completing time-and-motion studies for commercial clients. In addition to using local designers Frances Burke and Grant Featherston, the consultancy distributed Jens Risom furniture made under licence by William Latchford & Sons.

The stylish boardroom of Mono Pumps, showing *Lunar* fabric as curtains.

Lunar (1948)

Tiger Stripe in the office of founding professor of the University of Melbourne's Psychology Department,
Oscar Oeser (c. 1950). Described as 'undoubtedly brilliant, urbane and oftentimes charming,
Professor Oeser was a stylish dresser, with sophisticated tastes in art, music and architecture'.[36]

THE FINAL CURTAIN: CANBERRA CIVIC CENTRE THEATRE AND STATE LIBRARY OF VICTORIA

Between 1965 and 1967, despite residential work falling away, Burke delivered two major commissions for public spaces: a proscenium curtain for the Canberra Civic Centre Theatre (CCCT) and curtains for the new La Trobe Library and Irving Benson Hall at the State Library of Victoria. Both show similar development in the use of textural effects, indicating that Burke remained open to exploring new approaches in her design work.

Burke was the obvious person to deliver a contract the size of the CCCT, since she had an established reputation as a designer, connections with theatre suppliers and a history in collaborating with architects. Although this was a far larger project than she had previously completed, she had designed the interior of the Arrow Theatre, and provided curtains for the Eildon Theatre in 1951 and for smaller community theatres. According to Fabie Chamberlin, Burke was 'an avid first nighter',[37] so it is easy to imagine that she drew on her love of the theatre, the glamour of first nights and the anticipation of the moment the curtain rises into designing the striking curtains for audiences to contemplate while awaiting the performance.

The commission to design the proscenium curtains for the CCCT came via project architect Roy Simpson of the Melbourne practice Yuncken, Freeman Brothers, Griffiths & Simpson. The firm had completed stage one of the precinct in 1961—incorporating a large formal square, offices and library as one of the priority projects for the emerging national capital. Stage two featured a large theatre and smaller playhouse with a connecting foyer area. Sited adjacent to Capital Hill, one of the most important axes of Walter Burley Griffin's plan, the complex heralded a new level of confident modern public architecture for the city. The CCCT was mentioned by Simpson in his address as recipient of the 1997 RAIA Gold Medal as one of the three important place-making projects closest to his heart, and it is clear that he regarded collaboration with artists as central to the success of the overall scheme.

While admiring the architecture of the CCCT, Burke considered the interior of the theatre to be lacking in character:

> it was just about to be opened and they didn't know what to do about it. So, they called on me to design a proscenium curtain … and it worked. You know a theatre aperture in a full-sized theatre is a very big hole. It's a very big thing to design to … it's something you have to think about very hard … we wore … a trough in the ground running up and down from Melbourne to Canberra … trying to please the architects to such a point that at one stage I politely suggested that if they knew so much about textile design would they like to take the job on themselves

and do it. That finished the deal and I was left to get on and print 350 yards [for] the front face … [and supply] 350 yards to the lining and 350 yards to the backing so that when the curtain finally went up it carried nearly 1000 yards of material.[38]

The interiors may have indeed appeared stark: 'white bagged brick walls contrasting with the luxurious detailing of the white marble window frames and finely crafted timber joinery. The minimalist palette of the theatre interior set the stage for Burke's curtain to become the star of every show.'[39] Her design, a clever, arresting solution, worked beautifully from a distance when the curtains were closed, and its subtle variations of tone was a radical break from her characteristically structured designs. To create the full drop design of this size, with each motif measuring 122 by 86 centimetres, Burke applied a roller in loose gestures directly to the screens to obtain textural effects, one for each of the five colours. The combination of texture and layers of colour created the impression of peering into the centre of a fiery gem. The representation of flickering light 'was used to great effect by the lighting technicians' and was an inspired development of the theme established by artist Frank Hinder's gold mosaic columns in the adjoining Civic Square.[40] The theatre opened on 24 June 1965 with a gala performance of *Swan Lake* by the Australian Ballet—clearly a very glamorous night in the nation's capital:

> Flags, floodlights, fanfares … traffic cops, traffic snarls, distracted drivers … glamour gowns, fantastic furs, and a fine collection of white tie and tails … soul-satisfying music, brilliant dancing, applause, applause … Canberra had it all at the Theatre Centre's opening performance last night.[41]

The current senior curator at Canberra Museum and Gallery Virginia Rigney recalled the impact of this work:

> For a generation of Canberrans, the sense of anticipation as you waited in your seat for the show to begin, was joyfully complimented by Burke's curtain with its abstracted flaming orbs. As a child I recall the excitement of entering the lofty white spaces and the wide expanse of the theatre, but the curtain was the truly spectacular prelude to the delights that would soon appear.[42]

The curtain was removed from the theatre in the mid-1980s, and small samples of the original fabric were lodged in public collections. In 2020 a 17-metre-wide drop, in pristine condition, carefully rolled and stored in a cloth bag, was found in the roof of the technical offices of the theatre, allowing a vivid reassessment of the scale and achievement this work.

The CCCT is at the back of the square to the left of the image; *Ethos* by Tom Bass can be seen making her offering to the sun, as well as the pool with a fountain and a glimpse of the gold mosaic columns.

Black Opal (1965)

Black Opal in folds.

The interior of the Canberra Civic Centre Theatre showing Burke's proscenium curtain.

Shields curtain from the State Library of Victoria.

Two years after the completion of the CCCT, Burke was commissioned by the Victorian Department of Public Works to supply curtains for the newly built La Trobe Library at the State Library of Victoria. The new wing, designed to house the library's Australian research collection, replaced the temporary structure where coincidentally Burke had attended drawing classes at the Gallery School in 1933. This building included a purpose-built exhibition space named after library trustee and avid bibliophile Reverend Sir C Irving Benson who had been active in the area of public libraries for many years; the La Trobe Library and Irving Benson Hall opened in 1967.

The *Shields* design produced by Burke for this commission featured brown and black shield motifs on a white ground. The spaces between were infilled with textured areas in a putty colour, as if made with a brush, in a further exploration of textural mark-making. It is interesting to consider another coincidence: that Burke's business had been launched thirty years earlier when she had shown designs to Pierre Fornari at Georges, based on the drawings she had made in the ethnographic collections of the museum in the same building. Burke developed an enduring interest in Indigenous Australian design and delivered for the Irving Benson Hall a design that was possibly inspired by the museum's collections.

Architects were able to rely on Burke's aesthetic judgement, and her advice regarding the weight and texture of the base fabric, the appropriate design and the ideal colour for their interiors. Her designs and colours contributed to a balanced interior. Rather than seeking to draw all the attention and overwhelming the spaces in which they appeared, with the exception of her late commissions for public spaces, her approach to furnishing fabric was that it should be a single unit of a unified scheme.

As a committed modernist Burke believed that while design and colour gave pleasure, they also had the capacity to be socially instrumental, declaring 'it is time that artists came out of their ivory towers and applied their talents to improving community life. The best creative thought of the day should be applied to civic surroundings'.[43] In hospitals, baby health centres, factory canteens, workers' hostels and other institutional environments she gave considerable thought to the selection of designs and colours that responded appropriately to the setting and function, enhancing the mood of those who used them. The gestural mark-making that characterised her fabrics and the fact that they were handprinted humanised these spaces.

Overseas travel in the postwar period meant Burke was entirely up to date with international trends. Her passionate engagement with modern architecture, furniture and interior design meant she understood and communicated the aims of designers and architects; these collaborations positioned Burke as an acknowledged tastemaker in Australian modern design.

Irving Benson Hall showing curtains printed with dramatic shield motifs in black and brown punctuating the space, which was predominantly white and cream.

Indigenous influences:
Creating an image of modern Australia

Robin Boyd's criticism of the appropriation of Indigenous culture in Australia as a further injury following on from dispossession was perceptive:

> Where is this trend leading us? Will a national decorative form of lasting value develop or is this just an amusing fashion, the result of a search for 'new' Australian flavour to relieve the koalas and wattle? Meanwhile, what of the Aboriginal himself? First we take his land, then having altered as much as we can beyond all recognition, we take his art where he left off. Or has he left off?[44]

A decade earlier, leading Australian artist Margaret Preston had recommended that Australian designers use the forms, motifs and colours found in works by the nation's Indigenous people to create a modern national culture. She was not concerned with the embedded stories and rites in their implements, rock art, bark and body painting: 'please do not bother about what the carver meant in the way of myths, rites, etc.; that is not the decorators' affair'.[45] While Preston's encouragement did not lead to its popular uptake during the interwar period, interest in Indigenous culture by Australian designers including Burke increased during World War II, as they reflected on the nation as a geographic, political and cultural entity.

Increasingly engaged by modernism, Australian designers sought to position themselves and their work as international; however, at the same time they employed references to native flora and fauna as well as Indigenous culture and representations of Aboriginal people to distinguish their work as Australian and claim a connection to the land. In fact, most designers had very tenuous connections to land and Indigenous culture allowing them to problematically conflate flora, fauna and Indigenous people into a landscape that, while familiar to Australians as a set of visual tropes, was exotic and distant.

Burke's first Aboriginal-influenced design appears to be *Snake and Dugong* (1938–39), followed by *Rangga* (1940). The schematic nature of Burke's designs including *The Hunt* (1942), *Snake Totem* (c. 1940), *Boomerang* (c. 1950) and *Goanna* (c. 1954) suggests that bark paintings from Northern Australia were sources. In a 1949 article journalist Margaret Lawrence explained that 'Frances Burke is interested mainly in the aboriginal symbolic drawings, particularly those painted on bark sheets by northern Australian tribes'.[46]

The sources of Burke's designs extended beyond bark paintings. *Wuramu* (c. 1945–50) seems to derive from the mark-making traditions of the Yolŋu people of the Northern Territory and northern Western Australia, since their grave posts (*wuramu*) were often painted with strong geometric hatched-line designs. The motifs in *Bal* (c. 1945–51) appear to be influenced by the ceremonial body painting and pukumani poles of the people of the Tiwi Islands. Other designs whose names suggest Aboriginal sources, such as *Willy* (1945) and *Totem* (1952), are not easily explained because their motifs are so simple that they could be attributed to various sources.

While Burke became known for designs inspired by Indigenous culture, they constitute a relatively small percentage of her yardage designs. On the other hand, she frequently applied a range of such motifs to various smaller items such as tablecloths, tablemats, table napkins, handkerchiefs and tea towels over the period 1941–56. Many of these served as souvenirs purchased by American servicemen and women during World War II and as gifts for people overseas. She frequently used the figure of a man hunting a large crocodile, clearly appropriated from a Yolŋu bark painting from Gunbalanya, West Arnhem Land, in the collection of the National Museum of Victoria in Melbourne. In the postwar period, the production of decorative objects influenced by Indigenous cultures and representing Aboriginal people gained new impetus from the demand for souvenirs created by the 1956 Olympic Games held in Melbourne.

Boomerang (c. 1950)

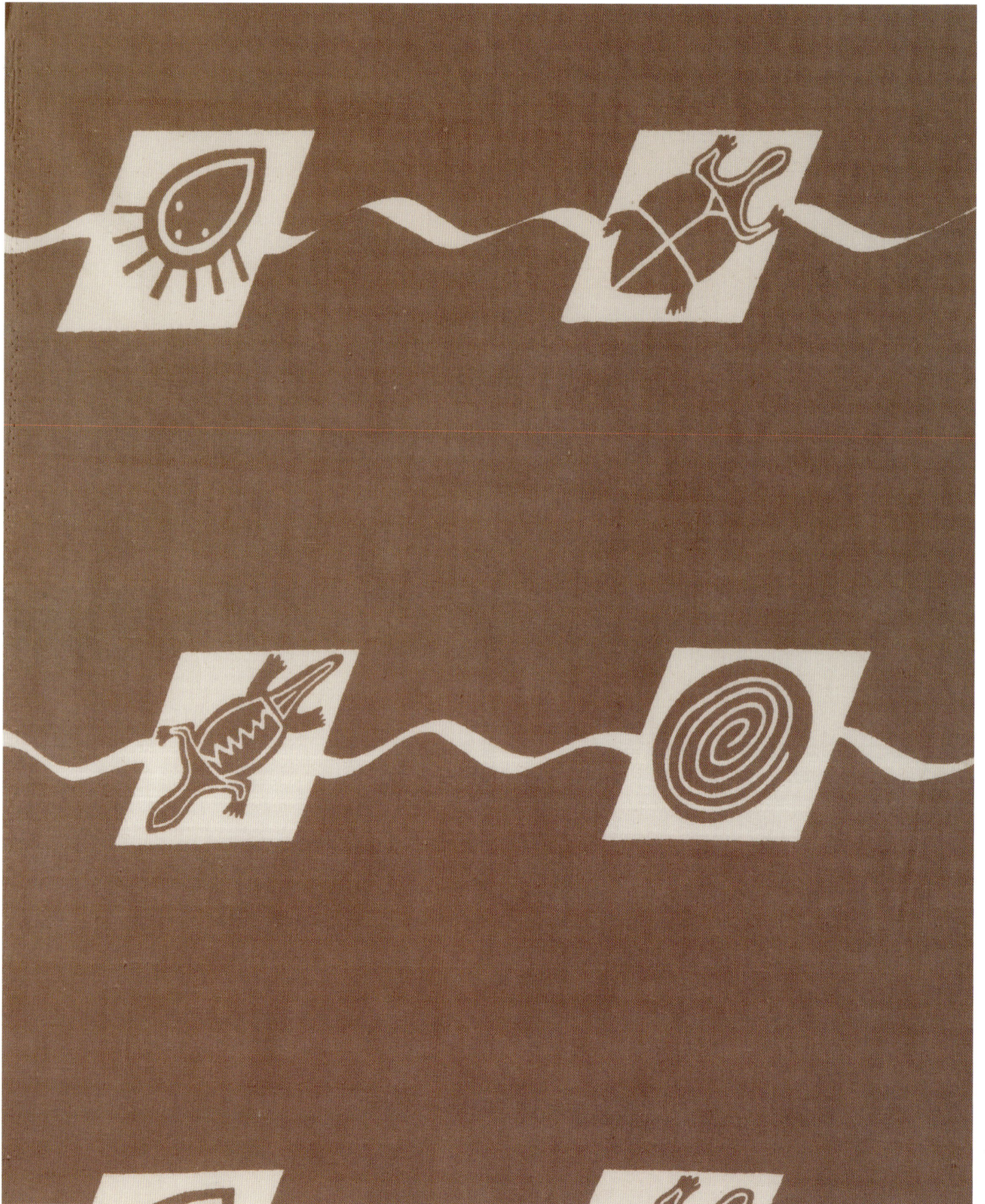

Goanna (c. 1954)

The Hunt (1942)

Snake and Dugong (c. 1939)

Crocodile and Hunter placemat (1950–55)

6

THE AUSTRALIAN POSTWAR HOME

A single bright colour and clean, simple linework printed on quality cotton or linen made Frances Burke's designs modern in style, instantly identifiable and very appealing. In addition to her arresting designs, Burke's ability to select and promptly supply orders with fabrics that were light-fast and wash-fast guaranteed that architects all over Australia, from the less well-known to the stellar, were happy to specify or recommend them.

With the end of World War II the feeling of freedom and a growing sense of optimism among young married couples led them to choose and create new ways of life that differed from their parents. Prospective homeowners sought simple open spaces that were affordable and met their need for a more informal way of life, often responding to the natural environment—the bush, the sea or river. As new homes were completed they required furnishing, and many young homeowners sought to fit out their homes with locally designed modern furniture and furnishings, as architectural historian Philip Goad wrote:

> In an architect-designed Los Angeles house, one expected to see furniture by Charles Eames, Eero Saarinen, George Nelson and perhaps an Isamu Noguchi coffee table. In Melbourne, one owned Grant Featherston, Douglas Snelling, Clement Meadmore furniture, Frances Burke fabrics and Arthur or Martin Boyd pottery.[1]

The Commonwealth Government's decisions to offer low-interest war service loans, to release land and pressure state governments to restrict house sizes while relaxing other building regulations, enabled a substantial increase in homeownership for the new generation. The resulting home-building boom meant that Burke was busy in the late 1940s and throughout the 1950s, with a growing list of residential projects. Her fabrics appeared in numerous architect-designed homes and were frequently documented in newspapers in all states and magazines with national distribution, notably *Australian Home Beautiful* and *Australian House and Garden*. Whether Burke's fabrics were specified by the architects and designers or chosen by clients who wanted contemporary furnishings is often unclear, but as architect and commentator Neil Clerehan reiterated, 'when the time came to furnish these new rooms, the appropriate components were already available: Featherston chairs, cork tiled floors, Frances Burke prints'.[2]

In the Balwyn house they built themselves over eighteen months, Rhonda and Herbert Hester chose Burke's *Bird and Tree* for the curtains and Clement Meadmore's white corded chairs.

VICTORIA

Architects Phyllis and John Murphy set up a successful home-based practice in two rooms of the Murphy family home in East Malvern in 1949–50. Phyllis reported that Burke 'went out of her way to work with architects … Frances was an astute businesswoman, she would have understood that with the short-ages—there were opportunities … when we started in practice everything was short—it was terrible'.[3] As interior design was not part of the Murphys' practice they did not specify Burke's fabrics but they certainly made suggestions for their clients' consideration, and they chose her fabrics for their own office and home, where clients would have seen their impact.

Peter McIntyre studied with the Murphys at the University of Melbourne's Faculty of Architecture. When interviewed in his Kew office, he recalled that he 'immediately started using Frances, and all the young architects did' when he commenced practice in 1950.[4] McIntyre went further than making sugges-tions, he recalled taking clients directly to Burke's showroom for consultations. Before graduating he had worked as Robin Boyd's assistant, managing a range of projects including the unforgettable House of Tomorrow, where Burke's fabrics were admired and for which Boyd's choice of colour had been the talk of the town.

A house designed by Boyd in the early 1950s, showing a similar delight in colour and a prominent use of Burke fabrics, was the Dunstan House in the Melbourne suburb of Balwyn. A window wall with white-painted wooden frames was hung with curtains in slate-blue *Wavy Stripe* coordinating with wall panels in ice blue and contrasting with 'flame red' ceiling panels. The main bedroom, with grey carpet and blue-grey walls, had a 'jonquil-yellow linen bedspread' and 'arresting "hot pink"

John and Phyllis Murphy chose *The Hunt* in orange for their home office.

Tartan fabric in different colours from those selected by John and Phyllis Murphy.

Phyllis Murphy, pictured in the sitting room, chose *Tartan* in green, blue and grey for the covers of the divans, which were transformed into the Murphys' bed at night.

curtains and cushions', as reported by Lesley Stahle, wife of architect Ross Stahle.[5]

Numerous articles in popular magazines featured Burke's fabrics lending their vibrant colour and contemporary style to the emerging vernacular of Australian postwar architecture. With designs for small houses incorporating a free flow between indoors and outdoors there was a blurring between the concept of 'holiday house' and 'suburban house', with the subtle simplicity of Burke's single-colour designs contributing to their sense of informality.

Burke's working relationship with Roy Grounds resumed in the early 1950s with two important residential projects located in spectacular positions. The first was the 1951–52 Ashton house Iluka on Beleura Hill, Mornington, overlooking the broad sweep of Port Phillip Bay, from Melbourne to The Heads. This was one of Grounds' most significant early postwar houses, for which he selected Burke's fabric *Oak Leaf Stripe* for curtaining the three floors of north-west facing windows.

The exterior of the Harman Portsea holiday house—the exterior colour flags the liberal use of colour in the interior.

Curtains in chartreuse *Oak Leaf Stripe* in the Harman holiday house, designed by architect Rae Featherstone in 1953. Sited at Portsea, the exclusive beach resort on the southern tip of the Mornington Peninsula, it was an influential holiday house design in terms of its spaces, style, colours and furnishings.

Oak Leaf Stripe, an interesting mix of oak leaves and stripes, similar to *Tiger Stripe,* was approved by architect Roy Grounds and clearly appreciated by Mr and Mrs Ashton for their house Iluka.

Oak Leaf Stripe (c. 1950).

The second of these projects, in 1953, was a house for lawyer and academic Dr Hans Leyser and his wife Joan, a journalist who wrote regularly on architecture and interior design for *Australian Home Beautiful*. Located in Kew and described as sitting like 'a delicate leaf on a sloping hillside that overlooks a wooded national park and golf links, Roy Grounds triangular shaped house is logically angled to its site'.[6] The house had a unified colour scheme intended to integrate it with its landscape, the 'study area and the other walls are painted a deeper shade of the exterior grey-green, and the windows are hung with grey-green and white patterned curtains by Frances Burke, their simplicity a unit contributing to the whole'.[7]

Squares (1951)

Joan and Hans Leyser chose *Squares* in a deep grey-green for the curtains, blending with the living room walls, for the house designed by Roy Grounds, known as the Triangular House.

Architect Ivor McInnes and his wife Beth Thwaites, a journalist for *The Argus*, designed their own house in riverside Lower Plenty. In 1953 the area, recently populated with dairy farms and orchards, was being transformed into an outer suburb of Melbourne. The house, Horizons, and its setting were described as a suburban idyll where the owners enjoyed entertaining friends, 'who are likely to turn up in numbers for conversation and good cheer, as well as a breath of the bush and a swim in the river in summer. There is a small landing stage and a springboard, comfortable chairs, and a barbeque under the trees.'[8]

The living and dining room decorated in a high-toned palette of yellows and blue featured a 'plate glass wall' of windows, with curtains in Burke's Wedgwood blue *Tiger Stripe* fabric framing an elevated, long view over the river and out towards the developing suburb.

Another house built in Lower Plenty in 1953—the product of architectural designer and mudbrick enthusiast Alistair Knox and the owner, artist Lindsay Edward—also featured *Tiger Stripe* to great effect. The restrained interior's older-style chairs were upholstered in the same contemporary blue fabric as the McInnes's house, with cushions in a contrasting red.

Tiger Stripe was clearly a popular design for both curtains and upholstery, appearing in countless Australian interiors of the postwar period. Selected for the home of Mr and Mrs W Krauss in the suburb of Glen Iris, which was designed by Polish émigré architect Kurt L Elsner in 1953, it was used to cover an older-style chair which created a striking focus for the living room. In the den, another Burke fabric, *Crete*, was used for curtains and the upholstery of a European-style divan bed; while curtains in the kitchen were in Burke's *Hispano*.

Tiger Stripe, used for curtains in the dining room of the McInnes's house in Lower Plenty, was also used in the living room.

The spare, peaceful interior of Lindsay Edward's house with blue *Tiger Stripe* upholstered chairs in the sitting room.

✝ comfort

by ALMA SOMERS

*Simple planning here pays off in sophisti-
cated effect by the use of smart unconven-
tional wall treatments.*

This house of many unusual but practical features
is built of maize-coloured bricks on a sloping, slightly
irregular site in Allenby Avenue, Glen Iris, Victoria.
Designed by architect, K. Elsner, it is the home of Mr.
and Mrs. W. Krauss.

Ingenious grouping of the rooms makes for comfortable, easy living . . . the sleeping quarters are incorporated in one wing, the living section in another, both
completely private from the other and yet linked by an
outdoor living area. The utilities, kitchen, laundry,
and bathroom are grouped in one compact section.

A special feature of the design is the use of folding
doors. These are fitted with grooved glass and are used
at the main entrance where they extend the full width
of the hall and to the living room.

(Continued on Page 82)

Den (above) is compact, cosy . . . well-fitted with desk and
divan. (Below) Living room opens onto rear sun terrace and
dining area into den.

Mr and Mrs Krauss obviously enjoyed Burke's designs: *Tiger Stripe* and *Crete* were two of the three designs they selected.

Tiger Stripe became synonymous with Burke, appearing in her range over a thirty-year period.

Totem (1948) in the living room of the Dunne house.

Crete curtains in the Watt family holiday house at Sorrento, designed by architects Mockridge, Stahle & Mitchell in 1955. At the counter in the foreground is Lesley Stahle, Melbourne contributor for *Australian House and Garden*, who introduced Burke to Sydney contributor Peggy Hull in 1950.

Home to a disproportionately large number of young architects, Beaumaris is a bayside Melbourne suburb that still lacks a railway station and retains some unpaved roads at the behest of the residents. In the 1950s it gained status as a secret enclave. Beaumaris houses frequently featured in magazines of the time, and according to Goad:

> possess a sense of openness, of connection with the landscape and a sense of relaxed planning not dictated by conventional social norms. These are houses properly planned to take advantage of the sun and the block, and provision of space for children—sun galleries and playrooms … houses that epitomize Good Life Modernism.[9]

The 1955 Dunne house by architects Mockridge, Stahle & Mitchell—a fine example of this good-life modernism in Beaumaris—was designed to 'keep the picturesque old tea-trees and eucalypts which provided a ready-made natural garden, but still take advantage of the view'.[10] The informality of the house, 'which is colourful, carefree, compact',[11] was evident in the connection of the living room and adjoining kitchen through a server window. Both rooms combined strong reds and greens on the walls and cabinetry, with Burke's *Totem* in red the highlight, framing the view from the living room. Similarly, strong contrasting colours appeared in another Beaumaris house—the 1961 Gye house, designed by architect James Earle, with Burke's *Shields* fabric in a grey-green in the living–dining area contrasting with vermillion painted kitchen cupboards.

Owner Eve Gye, displaying an ease with modern design, chose the bold *Shields* design for her family living room and kitchen.

This design, *Crossways*, was true to Burke's vision, modern but not overwhelming the other elements in the space: unpainted brick walls, green painted woodwork. A room-divider curtain in a plain dyed russet colour was also supplied by Burke.

In 1962 architects Christian and Kenneth Macdonald designed a contemporary extension to their suburban house in Canterbury, Melbourne. Both had trained at the highly regarded Gordon Institute in Geelong. Jane Williams, a family friend of the Macdonalds and Burke's production manager of twenty-seven years, consulted on colour choices and measured up for the *Crossways* print curtains in a shade of brown called Yarra, which remain in situ at the time of writing. The business card accompanying the quote stated that it came through the contract division of Burke's soft furnishing service, which consulted on interiors, supplying technical advice and colour coordination.

Paperwork in Christian Macdonald's handwriting notated measurements of windows and yardage requirements calculated by Jane Williams, business partner of Burke and a Macdonald family friend.

The Bunning & Madden Clareville house interior showing *Loop Stripe*.

NEW SOUTH WALES

Unlike the clusters of modern houses designed by young architects in and around Melbourne that provided a ready market for Burke's fabrics, the Sydney scene was different. In the iconic Rose Seidler House in 1950 and other modern houses on the north shore of Sydney Harbour from Wahroonga to Turramurra, and Pymble, Killara to Lindfield, photographs show that there was less interest in patterned furnishing fabrics. Architects and owners chose either plain-coloured cotton or linen fabric, imported materials such as matchstick blinds and hessian, or sheer fabrics and single-coloured Thai silks. Textural effects were clearly preferred to team with walls of windows, featuring views into bush landscapes, or of exposed brick and stone. Oriental rugs on slate or wooden floors were usually the only pattern seen. Architect Harry Seidler considered that the mural at the Rose Seidler House, complemented by the carefully chosen primary colours of the kitchen cupboards and Butterfly chairs, was sufficient decoration.

Despite this, Burke had supplied Sydney retailers, including department store David Jones and stores run by interior designers, since the 1940s. When Marion Hall Best first established her business in Queen Street, Woollahra, Burke began supplying her, continuing when Hall Best also opened in Rowe Street, Sydney, where designers Margaret Jaye and Stephen Kalmar also had their shops. Levy's Interiors in Knox Street, Double Bay, and Joyce Tebbutt's showroom Cabana in North Sydney also carried Burke's fabrics. Buyers for the department stores and the owners and interior consultants of the smaller designer showrooms in these prestigious locations would not have found the space to carry Burke's fabrics unless there had been a significant demand.

Burke's fabrics do appear in photographs and articles about homes in beach locations, from Coogee, south of Sydney Harbour, to Palm Beach at the tip of the Barrenjoey Peninsula between Pittwater and the coast—an idyllic holiday location for the very smart and very wealthy. In 1950 artist Elaine Haxton used Burke fabrics to furnish a boathouse in Clareville on Pittwater that she occupied while her new home, designed by Arthur Baldwinson, was under construction.

Nearby was the Clareville house designed by prominent architect, urban planner and writer Walter Bunning of the partnership Bunning & Madden, which had curtains of Burke's striking *Loop Stripe* in the living room. This house was a fine example of Bunning's commitment to modern architecture suiting the Australian environment, about which he wrote in his 1945 treatise *Homes in the Sun*; its impact was still recognised in 1953, as noted in an Australian government publication:

One of Sydney's show places is a luxury out-of-town house at Newport, on the Palm Beach Peninsula, some 20 miles north of the city … Built on a curve to follow the contours of hillside and beach, this sandstone house … takes full advantage of the scenic beauty of the landlocked waters on three sides … on the upper verandah, one has something of the feeling of being on board a yacht.[12]

A 1954 addition to a house in the seaside suburb of Coogee, designed by architects Basil Beirman and RS Clarke for Mr and Mrs W Short, was furnished by interior decorator Margaret Lord. Interior furnishings for the 'party room' included Burke's *Crete* in grey on white for the curtains and *Tiger Stripe* for the divan, which was adorned with cushions in orange, black and white featuring a horse motif.[13] *Tiger Stripe* was also used as chair covering in a Neutral Bay house redesigned by German émigré architect Hugh Buhrich in 1955. For the living room that looked out onto a pergola-covered terrace, curtains featuring Burke's *Squares* design were used to frame the view.

Burke's fabrics also appeared in photos of Warrimoo, the stylish country retreat in the Blue Mountains outside Sydney belonging to her friends Beryl Guertner and partner Kate Wormall. Howard Tanner, architect and friend of Guertner, who was the founding editor, in 1948, of the influential *Australian House and Garden*, recorded that under Guertner's editorship the magazine had 'in the era of self-help, opened up the possibilities of living with style on modest means … provided ingenious small-home plans … conveyed the excitement of good design, and promoted innovative paint colours and decorative schemes'.[14]

Guertner featured Burke's textiles in many issues of *Australian House and Garden*, giving her significant exposure. She chose *The Hunt* for a bedcover in her own home in Bad Black or charcoal for the predominantly white room, which sparkled with accents of pink and yellow, of which the lampshade in *Polka Dot* design was one.

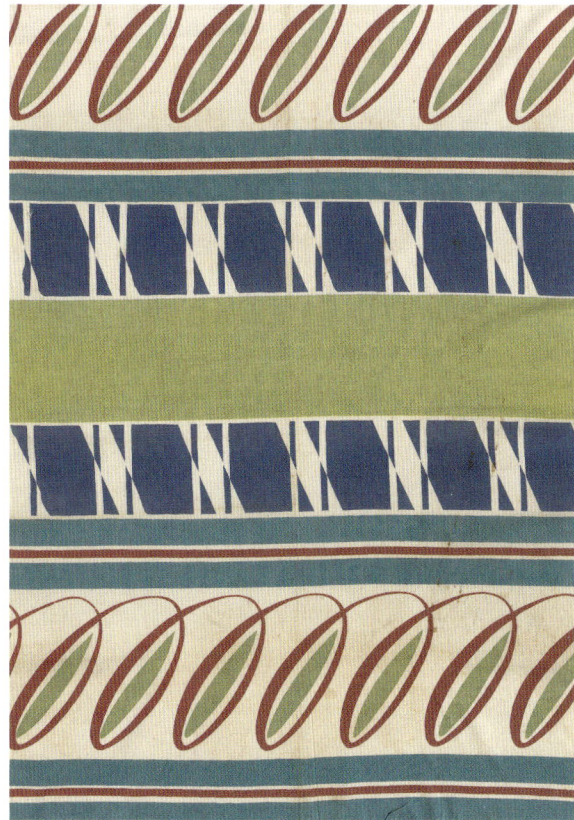

Loop Stripe (1948)

The Hunt and *Polka Dot* in the bedroom of the Guertner house, Warrimoo.

The living room of architect Vitaly Gzell's family house in Toowong, Brisbane, with built-in furniture and *Tiger Stripe* fabric.

QUEENSLAND

In his influential publication *Sub-tropical Housing* published in 1944, architect and lecturer Karl Langer wrote and presented house plans addressing tropical and subtropical climates of the more densely populated areas of Queensland, specifically to reduce the fatigue of housewives living and working in homes that were not airconditioned and seeking to rectify the perceived problems of glare.[15] Langer offered a new set of technical solutions to the situation that had produced the 'Queenslander', the vernacular timber home on stilts surrounded by verandahs, its picturesque fretwork providing privacy and allowing breezes to move through its dark interiors. His plans removed verandas and stilts, offering open living spaces, efficient kitchens and seamless connection with the outdoors. This was a change from the experience of a standard Queenslander, where nature was a spectacle viewed from above.

Many of the modern postwar homes in the Brisbane suburb of St Lucia were designed by architects who took up Langer's recommendations. In *Australia's Home* published in 1952, Robin Boyd explained how architects were building there because it was cheap, wooded, only 3 miles from the city, and had hilly slopes offering views over the Brisbane River. In addition to their modern plans and approach to materials, Boyd applauded their experimental use of colour—the external brickwork of the homes was painted in the Victorian tradition: 'White, blinding in Queensland's sun, was rarely used. Pale pinks, greys, light and dark olive greens in broad floods of paint soon made St

The postwar trend of beach houses employing strong colours and contrasts can be seen in Mr and Mrs W Hart's Mermaid Beach holiday house, designed by architect Jerry Trude, where curtains in bright yellow *Crete* contribute to the holiday atmosphere.

The striking wall colour in the dining room of architect David Bell's own house in St Lucia, Brisbane, boldly offsets Burke's *Oak Leaf* design in curtains and Snelling dining chairs and table.

Lucia one of Australia's most colourful suburbs.'[16] Architects who built in the neighbourhood included Karl Langer, Peter Newell, Edwin Hayes and Campbell Scott, Vitaly Gzell, Gordon Banfield and David Bell.

Already five years old when it was described by *Australian House and Garden* in 1954 as a 'pacemaker' house, the Gzell house at Toowong, a suburb adjoining St Lucia, featured exposed brick walls, built-in furniture, a fireplace and clay floor tiles. The use of pony-skin upholstery and floor covering in the living room provided another natural feature against which Burke's *Tiger Stripe* was used to dramatic effect for the substantial floor-to-ceiling windows.

Like the Gzell house and in contrast to the Queensland tradition of timber construction, David Bell, in designing his own house at St Lucia in 1955, also used plaster-clad brick walls, enabling the use of strong colours for the interiors. In the dining room, for example, deep red-brown walls provided a vivid backdrop for curtains in Burke's *Oak Leaf* in bright blue and Snelling chairs featuring brilliant green-coloured webbing. In architect Jerry Trude's own home, a renovated Victorian house in Toowong, the architect used bright and contrasting colours including tan, chartreuse and blue in a boys' bedroom, with bedcovers made of Burke's fabric *The Hunt*.[17]

Australian Home Beautiful chose Jack Harrison's house for the cover in April 1956, presenting an artfully styled image featuring Harrison, his family, friends and *Totem* fabric.

WESTERN AUSTRALIA

The West Australian capital Perth, with its coastal location and broad, swift-flowing Swan River, enables many of its residents to orient their homes to a water view. Due to the postwar material shortages lasting longer there than in other Australian cities, home building lagged, but the delay meant that modern design had a greater impact than in some other state capitals. One of Western Australia's most distinguished and awarded architects of the modern movement, Mervyn Parry, both designed and (experimentally) acted as builder for the 1955 Smith house in Claremont, referred to by the West Australian Institute of Architects as 'an outstanding home'. Setting the trend in the use of strong colours, the Smiths chose Burke's *Loop* design

in charcoal and burnt orange on a white ground fabric against charcoal-coloured walls for their living room.

Burke's fabrics were also chosen for another notable Perth house, this one located at City Beach. Designed for Jack Harrison, the eminent musician, to take advantage of spectacular views of the Indian Ocean, the home, with its striking exterior marine-blue concrete walls and red and yellow exterior doors, was an early private commission for émigré architect Iwan Iwanoff in 1955. The use of primary colours continued through the interior where floor-to-ceiling curtains of *Totem* fabric in blue provided an almost seamless link to sky and sea.

Colour is the magic wand that transforms the good modern lines of this house and make it an outstanding home.

Good design, planning and colour, earmark the home of Mr. and Mrs. Howard Smith as a vital indication of the trend of modern architecture in West Australia. Keyed to contemporary living, it is the result of smooth co-ordination between architect Mervyn Parry, Mr. E. Ireland, who designed and made all the fitments, and the home-owners, who feel that their new home is exactly right for them.

Uncommon and extremely functional distribution of the plan places the entrance hall to the back of the house. The entrance is sheltered by the extended roof line of a car-port. A deep blue door opens into the small entrance hall, made important by colour and a beautiful stairway leading to the upper floor. White-washed brick walls, oyster stair rail and blue ceiling are coolly complimented by red baked brick tile flooring and Kingfisher blue and oyster stair carpet.

Charcoal walls hit a strong colour note in the lounge-dining room, and allow a blending of more brilliant colours in furnishing and accents.

(continued on page 78)

The Smith house, Claremont, with *Loop* in charcoal and burnt orange for a living room; in this case a colour image would have shown a striking combination.

The unusual shaped living room of the Kuring house where *Wavy Stripe* had been used in a small space to great effect.

SOUTH AUSTRALIA

South Australia's capital, Adelaide, sits between the sea and the Mount Lofty Ranges. In the foothills of the ranges a ribbon of bush-garden suburbs had developed, offering the opportunity of infill development in the postwar period. The Kuring and Honey houses, designed by Hassell & McConnell in 1955, were located on a single narrow block of land in Netherby and were cleverly designed to complement one another. Then twenty years into his career, Colin Hassell had spent time in London before the war, surrounded by 'the fervor of modernism and the teachings of the Bauhaus',[18] which led him to experiment with butterfly roofs, broad eaves to shield the north-facing floor-to-ceiling windows and some quirky, irregular-shaped rooms. In the living room of the Kuring house, Burke's *Wavy Stripe* fabric was used for floor to ceiling windows windows and glass

sliding doors that looked onto a paved terrace and garden.

Views to the outdoors were important to South Australian artist Ruth Tuck, who had studied painting under Dorrit Black, and Tuck's husband, architect and artist Mervyn Smith. For the family home in Fullarton the couple purchased two of Burke's fabrics: *Totem* in chartreuse, which was used for curtains, and *Crete,* in blue, which was used in the bedroom as a divider-curtain to cover racks of completed paintings. These fabrics were purchased in the late 1940s, later providing inspiration for Tuck in landscape and botanical works painted when staying at Port Elliot, on the Fleurieu Peninsula south of Adelaide. Tuck's watercolours incorporated faithful renditions in both scale and colour of Burke's fabrics, framing charming domestic views through windows to the sea and gardens.

Totem seen in a 1985 painting by Ruth Tuck titled *Birthday Flowers*.

REPOSITIONING THE BUSINESS

Many Australian architect-designed postwar homes were set in new suburbs at the edge of capital cities, ideally with water views and if not, with access to other natural landscape features. Local architects inspired by the modern design pioneered in Europe prior to the war and then in the United States responded to the Australian settings and local climates. In doing so they frequently borrowed from the holiday house as a type, since it offered a potent, 'suggestive image of a freer life in an apparent natural paradise, economically and physically available to everyone … A local version of the promised freedoms of early European architectural modernism seen right here; "the good life"—perhaps one spent permanently on holiday'.[19]

Burke's graphic fabric designs, their white lines slicing throught a single strong colour, offered a coherent modern look that was considered desirable for nearly three decades from the late 1930s to the late 1960s. Specific designs including the perennially popular *Tiger Stripe,* in addition to *Totem, Crete* and *Wavy Stripe,* were seen in an extensive range of settings, in houses across the spectrum, from affluent to modest.

Burke's residential orders had declined by the mid-1960s, the popularity of her designs overtaken by the cycle of contemporary furnishing trends. At an event Burke organised for trade representatives in April 1967 she announced a re-positioning of the business. Although she would continue to supply the most popular designs in the Frances Burke Fabrics range, printing to order 'if the job was big enough', she now styled herself as a consultant designer/decorator. As part of the service she would source fabrics from department stores and other shops, and provide colour advice. Although phrased slightly differently, the core of Burke's message had essentially not changed in thirty years and it was still relevant:

> Fabric design … must be functional, decorative and architectural: it must fit in with our way of life and architecture. A fabric is just one factor in the furnishing of a room, and it should be designed to suit exactly. Properly selected, pattern can confirm the character of a room, enhance its style, reflect its purpose and fit in appropriately with its size, whether this is as small as a flat kitchen or as big as a ballroom.[20]

Abstract designs

Abstract designs became an increasingly important part of Burke's oeuvre in the postwar period. Some were loosely derived from Indigenous culture or were intended to be understood as such, including *Churinga* (1946) and *Totem* (1948). In these designs Burke isolated a single motif, divorced from its storytelling and symbolic context, and treated it as purely decorative. It was only through naming that the connection of these designs to their origins were acknowledged.

Western decorative traditions were the basis of a number of abstract designs, including *Tartan* (1948), *Wavy Stripe* (1950), *Polka Dot* (c. 1952) and versions of the diamond-shaped harlequin design—as in *Harlequin* (1950) and the closely related *Crystals* (1959). Belying their historic origins these designs were given a modern twist each time. The lines of tartans were hand drawn rather than straight and the spacing between them unpredictable. *Polka Dot* was larger than a traditional coin spot, and the diamond designs were conversely smaller and incorporated additional decorative touches such as the stamen-like elements in both *Harlequin* and *Crystals*.

Burke's most successful abstract design in terms of sales and longevity was *Tiger Stripe* (1938). It was based on the pelt of the big cat according to its title but was influenced by Michael O'Connell's *Wavy Stripe* (1933) which, in various versions, suggested natural sources including sand dunes, the lines made by waves and the ribbon-like layers of metamorphic rock formations. Burke's version was sleeker and more modern—a reverse design with white lines showing through the printed colour, and with a less ambiguous source. *Tiger Stripe* was printed continuously throughout the more than three decades of her career, in a large range of colours, becoming a favourite of interior designers as well as the general public.

Other abstract designs developed by Burke in the postwar period inspired by nature include *Lunar* (1948), which suggests a full moon in a cloudy sky; *Crossways* (1962) and *Reflections* (1955), which may have been inspired by the early abstractions of Dutch artist Piet Mondrian who had explored a range of approaches to transforming his observations of reflections on water into abstract works on canvas. If so, this was an approach she shared with her friend and colleague, furniture designer Clement Meadmore, who used mosaic tiles on tabletops inspired by Mondrian's work around this time.

In addition to Indigenous and natural sources, Burke developed abstract designs in response to the work of contemporary designers from other fields, such as the stark, reductivist geometric lines of the steel furniture produced by Meadmore and American designers Harry Bertoia and Charles and Ray Eames. Examples of this inspiration from contemporary metal furniture and architectural design appear in *Pacifica* (1953), *Links* (1955), *Staccato* (1962) and *Craze* (1948).

Totem (1948)

Harlequin (1950)

Craze (1948)

Reflections (1955)

Links (1955)

A LIFE
BY DESIGN

Burke drew inspiration from shells in her early designs and continued
to collect and paint them over the years.

A relaxed and carefree Burke on Anglesea beach.

n the late 1960s Frances Burke was, in all probability, feeling that the demands of her thirty-year commitment to her business were enough. So she closed the doors in 1970, which meant she had more time to return to her first love, painting, and devote her considerable energy to various local, national and international design, art and craft organisations. Her involvement was either in a formal capacity, as a board or founding member, or on an informal basis as an advocate and ambassador. She travelled frequently, reporting her observations and ideas, giving talks and lectures to neighbourhood and community groups, university associations, and art and design interest groups.

From the late 1940s Burke had been an authoritative advocate for 'good design' and design as a professional practice, her opinion frequently sought by the media. Widely acknowledged towards the end of her life, Burke was able to bask in the glow of a successful career at the same time as actively supporting younger artists and designers with discreet financial contributions and by talking up their achievements.

Having joined the Victorian Arts and Crafts Society shortly after establishing her business, Burke became an active member, exhibiting in most of the Arts and Crafts Society shows between 1938 and 1965. In 1968 Burke was elected president of the society and travelled to the World Craft Council's Biennial Assembly in Lima, Peru, as one of the Australian representatives. In 1972 she travelled to Samarkand, Uzbekistan, again as the society's president representing Australia.

Another organisation Burke had a long association with was the Contemporary Arts Society (CAS). She joined as a founding member in 1938. Established by George Bell, the CAS rejected the deep-seated conservatism of Victorian art institutions and moves by Prime Minister Menzies to establish an Australian Academy of Art modelled on the Royal Academy in London. After a hiatus of seven years, when the CAS ceased to operate, former president John Reed and gallery owner and restaurateur Georges Mora revived it in 1954, establishing its headquarters in 1956 at the newly founded

A Burke painting capturing the dramatic coast near Anglesea, where her holiday house was located.

Museum of Modern Art and Design of Australia (MOMAD). Burke was an early member of the group formed to set up MOMAD in Melbourne, and had lobbied successfully to include design in the title. She also insisted that the organisation hold regular exhibitions of design, and by 1958 was a member of the governing council. MOMAD operated until 1966. During this eight-year period Burke remained an active member, exhibiting, lending objects and opening exhibitions.

Burke was the only female member of the Society of Designers for Industry (SDI) in 1947, which included Richard ('Jimmy') Haughton James, Max Forbes, Grant Featherston, Fred Ward, Ron Rosenfeldt, William Falconer Green, Selwyn Coffey, Scorgie Anderson and Charles Furey. In 1956, when Melbourne hosted the Olympic Games, members of the SDI including Burke were involved as both organisers and exhibitors in the accompanying Fine Arts Exhibition of the Cultural Olympics. Industrial design, which included textile design, was shown at Storey Hall, Royal Melbourne Technical College. In 1983, almost forty years since she joined the SDI, Burke was inducted as a Life Fellow of the organisation now known as the Design Institute of Australia (DIA). In 1998 she was inducted into the DIA Hall of Fame.

On 1 January 1970, the same year that Burke closed her business, she was awarded an MBE, becoming a Member of the Order of the British Empire (Civil Division), for services to the textile industry, art and design, the first and only Australian textile designer to be honoured in this way. An MBE is awarded to people who have a national profile in their chosen area based on 'outstanding achievement or service to the community'. The investiture was made at Government House, Melbourne, by Queen Elizabeth II, an event that gave Burke great pleasure; she retained the very many letters of congratulation she received.

Together with close friend Maie Casey, Burke held a number of exhibitions, including one in 1979 at the Lyceum Club in Melbourne, where she exhibited drawings, paintings and monoprints. She had also produced illustrations for Casey's volumes of poetry: *Verses by Maie Casey* (1963) and *From the Night* (1976), and then supplied the cover for *Rare Encounters* (1980), Maie's personal observations of people she had met during her years in public life.

Burke's return to her art practice encouraged her to engage with new arts organisations, becoming a foundation member of the National Print Council in 1971. Later she joined its committee, putting forward recommendations for art prizes for printmakers and the institutions that sponsored them.

In celebration of the 1975 International Women's Year, Burke was invited by the federal government, as a 'pioneer of contemporary design', to a reception on Friday 7 March at the Customs House in Melbourne to honour 'Women Firsts'. This was a particularly pertinent accolade, as in the preceding forty years she had become a remarkable designer, principal of

A medal awarded to Burke when she became a Member of the Order of the British Empire in 1970.

On her return from a trade fair in Osaka, Japan in the early 1960s, Burke was presented as a design expert. This kind of publicity facilitated her shift to a public role as an advocate for design.

An installation from the Art Gallery of South Australia showing Burke's *Shields* design (1965) with a Douglas Snelling chest of drawers (c. 1952), an Elaine Haxton painting—*Figure with Shell and Fish* (c. 1952)—and an Alex Leckie double-spouted face urn (c. 1961) shown with works by two Japanese ceramicists.

A National Gallery of Australia poster for a substantial exhibition celebrating Australia's Bicentenary: Australian Decorative Arts 1788–1988. The poster showed the Burke design *Rangga* (1941), a Schulim Krimper bookcase (c. 1949), a Helge Larsen and Darani Lewers coffee set (1971) and a Harold Hughan large Iris series bowl.

a successful design business and spokesperson for design, seeing it as critical to the success of Australian manufacturing.

Burke's longest organisational commitment was to RMIT, where she began her classes in 1933. Shortly after she had finished her studies in Applied Design in 1937, Burke entered an informal arrangement with the school—she gave advice, judged exams and competitions, and assisted with curriculum development. Later this arrangement was formalised with membership of the Course Advisory Committee of the School of Art, which continued until 1986.

After sustaining injuries in a car accident in East Melbourne in 1986, Burke channelled her energy into convalescing, and her hands-on period of professional involvement and her advocacies had come to an end. However, in June 1987 Burke was awarded the first Honorary Doctorate of Arts conferred by the Faculty of Art at RMIT. In his address Colin Barrie, foundation dean, expressed how even 'in her retirement her continued interest in and commitment to the importance of design has been remarkable. She has been notable in her support of and her interest in the younger generation.'[1]

Burke, who was unable to attend as she was still recuperating, had written her doctoral acceptance speech and the keynote speech, both of which Barrie delivered. In it she reiterated the need for the younger graduating students to have:

> the wonderful opportunities at RMIT that I had …
> You are well aware that learning is a life-long process
> and I urge every one of you to keep closely in touch
> with this Institute. I can only say that over the years
> I have derived great pleasure and satisfaction by my
> close involvement with the Faculty of Art.[2]

The keynote speech Burke was invited to give was a message to the graduates:

> To you who are about to commence your life's work,
> go forth with the knowledge that my generation has
> implicit faith in you. You, [are] the real resources of
> the nation. Australia has yet to see more clearly its
> role and contribution to the betterment of the family
> of man and it will do so only by creating a climate of
> opportunity in which the richness of the minds of
> its youth and its people can fully flower. A climate
> of tolerance, compassion, inventiveness, adventure,
> enterprise and flexible but long-term planning. As
> Woodrow Wilson once said: 'by the scale of your
> hemisphere shape your designs.' You, with care, will
> develop the arts and sciences and in this great south
> land on the new centre line of the world will contribute
> to the foundation of its genius loci.[3]

By this time anyone involved in art, craft or design, not to mention the broader general public, would have heard of, read about or seen Burke and her fabrics; her name was synonymous with self-assured, distinctive work printed in her signature strong, vibrant colours. She had achieved success and influence; she had become a household name.

In her 'Two Year Plan for Living', written before her business was established, Burke explored the avenues her life might take.[4] She noted that there was an 'urgency of getting a congenial job', accompanied by 'an attitude of mind that made for security— hope and ambition' and that she needed 'an objective'. She listed 'unhampered living conditions in pleasant surroundings, a collection of friends likely to be part of this development' and wrote that she needed 'substantial interest and affection', but 'all depended on securing a congenial job, ability to hold it— sincerity in developing it'. She listed her 'assets for application' as 'necessity—genuine ability to design, average intelligence in learning and execution capacity'. She also asked for a 'clear head and clear vision … peace happiness [and] security'. By all accounts Burke had been spectacularly successful in designing her life, in understanding herself, her needs and abilities, in making plans and fulfilling them.

Burke's own words from a 1952 interview indicate that she certainly felt successful:

> Some of my colleagues from the art world chip me
> about having developed into a 'monster of commerce'
> … I make no secret of the fact that I appreciate money,
> because it enables you to live with grace and dignity.
>
> You might think that, for a person with artistic
> leanings, my life of designing, printing, producing,
> and selling fabrics has been unspectacular.
>
> But it's been deeply satisfying to me, because I've
> felt I've been supplying an artistic need in the community and bringing sound artistic values into the familiar
> sphere of ordinary everyday life. I might have starved if
> I'd stayed at an easel without being able to do any good
> for anybody. I've always been able to separate essentials
> from non-essentials pretty quickly. I think that faculty
> helps a person score bull's-eyes in life.[5]

The financial security generated from her business and well-managed real estate investments enabled Burke and Chamberlin to live and entertain in their East Melbourne house, and to continue enjoying their circle of friends into the last years of their life together. After a period of illness in 1994 Burke died of pneumonia in Caritas Christi Hospice, Kew, on 14 October, ending a working life of fifty years and a companionship lasting sixty-seven years.

In the late 1940s Burke's fabric *Totem* was used for curtains in the north-facing dining room at Buda House museum, Castlemaine Victoria. In 2005 the originals, in a fragile state, were reluctantly removed by the curator. In 2020 a roll of original *Totem* fabric in the same colour was serendipitously located by a collector, who contacted the authors via Instagram. The new curtains in this fabric are now installed at Buda.

Epilogue

In 1998 Fabie Chamberlin, as Burke's executor, ensured that Burke's legacy as a textile designer lived on with the donation of $100 000 to the Textile Resource Centre located in the Department of Fashion and Textile Design at RMIT.

The Textile Resource Centre, which had been established in 1994 to research and communicate Australia's fashion and textile history, was the outcome of both international research undertaken by Associate Professor Janet Medd, head of the Department of Fashion and Textile Design, and of a Master of Arts proposal from Robyn Oswald-Jacobs. Medd had previously investigated the potential of a university centre with this focus, and consequently was delighted to supervise the first Australian design history thesis in the faculty, a study into the life and work of Melbourne-based textile designer Frances Burke.

While a Commonwealth Department of Education, Employment and Training grant enabled the establishment of the centre and Oswald-Jacobs' appointment as manager, Chamberlin's donation enabled its expansion and led to the centre being named the Frances Burke Textile Resource Centre, by which it was known for twenty years.

The centre provided the foundation for the current RMIT Design Archives, which plays a vital role in actively collecting, researching and publishing on design in Melbourne.

Burway Prints studio manager Jane Williams, Frances Burke and an unidentifed man at the Anglesea holiday house in 1952.

Burke at Anglesea, where she loved exploring the natural world.

Notes

FOREWORD

1   Joel Sanders, 'Curtain wars: Architects, decorators, and the 20th-century modern interior', *Harvard Design Magazine*, vol. 16, 2002.

1   FINDING HER WAY

1   Anne Purves, interview by Robyn Oswald-Jacobs, 19 April 1994.
2   Marjorie Tipping, interview by Robyn Oswald-Jacobs, 14 November 1995.
3   Philip Jones, *Art & Life: The Memoir of a Man Bearing Witness to the Remarkable World of Heide* (Sydney: Allen & Unwin, 2004), p. 200.
4   Frances Burke, taken from twelve interviews by Robyn Oswald-Jacobs, February 1991 – February 1992.
5   Margaret Lord, *A Decorator's World* (Sydney & London: Ure Smith, 1969), p. 90.
6   Frances Burke, taken from twelve interviews by Robyn Oswald-Jacobs, February 1991 – February 1992.
7   ibid.
8   ibid.
9   'Police Court News', *Brunswick Leader*, 22 February 1918.
10 Fabie Chamberlin, interview by Robyn Oswald-Jacobs, 13 September 1995.
11 Diane Masters in conversation with Robyn Oswald-Jacobs, 1995.
12 Anne Purves, interview by Robyn Oswald-Jacobs, 19 April 1994.
13 Peter Di Scasio, 'Australian Lesbian Artists of the Early Twentieth Century' in *Out Here: Gay and Lesbian Perspectives VI*, eds Yorick Smaal & Graeme Willett (Melbourne: Monash University Publishing, 2011). Permission granted by Monash University Publishing.
14 Caroline Ambrus, *Australian Women Artists: First Fleet to 1945: History, Hearsay and Her Say* (Woden, ACT: Irrepressible Press), p. 161.
15 Frances Burke, Pioneering Design: 3 Decades of Design Development in Australia, lecture to the East Melbourne Historical Society (transcript), 21 April 1980.
16 Janine Burke, 'Sex and Ping Pong: Sidney Nolan and the Gallery School', https://findanexpert.unimelb.edu.au/news/2507-sex-and-ping-pong--sidney-nolan-and-the-gallery-school, 19 April 2017.
17 Frances Burke, Pioneering Design, lecture to the East Melbourne Historical Society (transcript), 21 April 1980.
18 Frances Burke, cited in June Helmer, *George Bell: The Art of Influence* (Melbourne: Greenhouse Publications, 1985), p. 17.
19 Maie Casey, opening speech, Exhibition of George Bell Paintings, Artarmon Galleries, 4 August 1971.
20 Mary Eagle and Jan Minchin, *The George Bell School: Students, Friends, Influences* (Melbourne & Sydney: Deustcher Art & Resolution Press, 1981).
21 Frances Burke, Pioneering Design, lecture to the East Melbourne Historical Society (transcript), 21 April 1980.
22 ibid.
23 Maie Casey, opening speech, Exhibition of George Bell Paintings, Artarmon Galleries, 4 August 1971.
24 Betty Blunden, interview by Robyn Oswald-Jacobs, 24 April 1995.
25 Jackie Dickenson, *Australian Women in Advertising in the Twentieth Century* (Basingstoke: Palgrave Macmillan, 2016), p. 81.
26 Betty Blunden, interview by Robyn Oswald-Jacobs, 24 April 1995.
27 Fabie Chamberlin, interview by Robyn Oswald-Jacobs, 13 September 1995.
28 Burke quoted in 'Crusader for Local Color', *People*, 24 September 1952, p. 19.
29 Harriet Edquist, *Michael O'Connell: The Lost Modernist* (Melbourne: Melbourne Books), p. 69.

2   FORGING A CAREER IN DESIGN

1   'Corroboree Fashions May Inspire Paris', *Herald*, 11 June 1937.
2   'Designing Fabrics', *Woman's World*, June (1940), p. 24.
3   Frances Burke, interview by Dimity Reed, 1980; Bob Quirk, 'Tribal Motifs Go Around the World', *Australasian Post*, 24 January 1952, p. 17.
4   Frances Burke, Pioneering Design, lecture to the East Melbourne Historical Society (transcript), 21 April 1980.
5   ibid.

6   RMIT Design Archives, Frances Burke 0004/2001, Box 1.
7   'Designing Fabrics', *Woman's World*, June (1940), p. 24.
8   'Hand Printed Linens: Novel Creations by Young Artist', *Herald*, 2 November 1937.
9   Yvonne Atkinson, in Mary Eagle and Jan Minchin, *The George Bell School: Students, Friends, Influences* (Melbourne & Sydney: Deutscher Art Publications & Resolution Press, 1981), p. 176.
10 Flocking involves treating with adhesive and dusting with fibres to create an absorbent surface.
11 Peter Cuffley, *Australian Houses of the Forties and Fifties* (Melbourne: Five Mile Press, 1993), p. 180.
12 Frances Burke, taken from twelve interviews by Robyn Oswald-Jacobs, February 1991 – February 1992.
13 Burke quoted in Fiona Capp, 'Award for Fabric Designer Who Captures Light and Life', *Age*, 8 June 1987.
14 Holloway's wall-hanging is in the collection of the National Gallery of Australia.
15 Joyce Storey, *Textile Printing* (London: Van Nostrand Reinhold Company, 1974), p. 107.
16 Frances Burke, taken from twelve interviews by Robyn Oswald-Jacobs, February 1991 – February 1992.
17 Anne Purves, interview by Robyn Oswald-Jacobs, 19 April 1994.
18 Frances Burke, Pioneering Design, lecture to the East Melbourne Historical Society (transcript), 21 April 1980.
19 'Crusader for Local Color', *People*, 24 September 1952, pp. 18–19.
20 'Hand Printed Linens: Novel Creations by Young Artist', *Herald*, 2 November 1937.
21 Frances Burke, taken from twelve interviews by Robyn Oswald-Jacobs, February 1991 – February 1992.
22 Janet Robinson, telephone interview by Robyn Oswald-Jacobs, 24 May 1995.
23 Margaret Lawrence, press release, Australian Textile Designers Work on Large Scale: Striking Designs by Frances Burke,1952.
24 Olga Drossinos, 'Summer Evening Dresses from Paris', *The Home: An Australian Quarterly*, 17, 1 (1936), p. 70.

3   DEVELOPING A NATIONAL MARKET

1   Laurie Carew, telephone interview by Robyn Oswald-Jacobs, 16 May 1995.
2   Paul Haefliger, 'Aboriginal Art', *Sydney Morning Herald*, 12 August 1941.
3   Editorial, 'Textiles From Japan: Dumping Effects Felt', *Age*, 12 September 1947.
4   Editorial, 'Crusader for Local Color', *People*, 24 September 1952, p. 19.
5   Elizabeth Street, 'The Life of Melbourne,' *Argus*, 4 September 1948.
6   David Crowther, telephone interview by Robyn Oswald-Jacobs, 20 September 1995.
7   Joan Leyser, 'They Took up the Challenge!', *Australian Home Beautiful*, 32, 5 (1953), p. 39.
8   Ted Worsley, interview by Robyn Oswald-Jacobs, 8 May 2019.
9   Joan Leyser, 'They Took up the Challenge!', *Australian Home Beautiful*, 32, 5 (1953), pp. 34–5, 37, 39. Duck is a medium-weight cotton fabric.
10 Beverley Graham (Knox), interview by Robyn Oswald-Jacobs, 10 March 1994.
11 John Rodriquez, interview by Robyn Oswald-Jacobs, 19 June 1994.
12 RMIT Design Archives, Bea (Bee) Taplin 0029/2011, Box 6.
13 Catriona Quinn, 'Margo's Interior Design Practice' (unpublished manuscript).
14 Claudio Alcorso, *The Wind You Say* (Sydney: Angus & Robertson, 1993), p. 63.
15 Claudio Alcorso, interview by Robyn Oswald-Jacobs, 11 July 1993.
16 Julie Petersen, 'The Name Will Live on After we are Gone', in Christina Sumner, Julie Petersen, Donna C Braye, *Australian Accent: The Designs of Annan Fabrics and Vandé Pottery in the '40s and '50s* (Sydney: Mosman Art Gallery).
17 ibid., p. 11.
18 Peter McNeil, 'Designing Women: Gender, Modernism and Interior Decoration in Sydney, c. 1920–1940', (master's thesis, Australian National University, 1993), p. 62.
19 Molly Grey, 'Wartime Furnishing in Australia', *Australia National Journal* (June–August, 1940), p. 62.
20 Margaret Lord, *A Decorator's World* (Sydney & London: Ure Smith, 1969), p. 96.
21 Marion Hall Best, 'Sydney Living Museums, Papers of Marion Hall Best 1935–1970', (unpublished memoir), MS31: MHB/A/1.

22 Margaret Lord, *Interior Decoration: A Guide to Furnishing the Australian Home* (Sydney: Ure Smith, 1944), p. 57.

23 Margaret Lord, *A Decorator's World* (Sydney & London: Ure Smith, 1969), p. 110.

24 Deirdre Broughton (Hall Best) cited in Michaela Richards, *The Best Style: Marion Hall Best and Australian Interior Design 1935–1975* (Sydney & New York: Art & Australia Books, 1993), p. 21.

25 Michaela Richards, *The Best Style* (Sydney & New York: Art & Australia Books, 1993), p. 29.

26 Marion Hall Best, 'Sydney Living Museums, Papers of Marion Hall Best 1935–1970', (unpublished memoir), MS31: MHB/A/1.

27 Daniel Thomas, cited in Michaela Richards, *The Best Style* (Sydney & New York: Art & Australia Books, 1993), p. 7.

28 Mollie G Wells, 'Hand-Printed Linens: Melbourne Artist's Work', *Sydney Morning Herald*, 17 February 1938.

29 *Argus*, 31 August 1955.

30 Fabie Chamberlin, interview by Robyn Oswald-Jacobs, 7 March 1995.

31 (Lady) Betty Grounds, interview by Robyn Oswald-Jacobs, 21 February 1991.

32 Genevieve Lansell, interview by Robyn Oswald-Jacobs, 25 January 2020.

33 Beverley Ednie, interview by Robyn Oswald-Jacobs and Nanette Carter, 31 July 2018.

34 *Herald*, 1 February 1938.

4 CREATING THE FRANCES BURKE BRAND

1   Michael Bogle, conversation with Robyn Oswald-Jacobs, Sydney, 23 July 2019.

2   'AWA advertisement', photograph by Max Dupain, *Australian House & Garden*, December 1949, p. 85.

3   Frances Burke, Pioneering Design, lecture to the East Melbourne Historical Society (transcript), 21 April 1980.

4   Caroline Miley, 'The Arts Among the Handicrafts: The Arts and Crafts Movement in Victoria 1889–1929', (PhD Thesis, La Trobe University, 1993), p. 9.

5   Editorial, 'Arts and Crafts Society', *Age*, 26 March 1938.

6   *Quarterly Bulletin of the Arts and Crafts Society*, October–November (1965), p. 3.

7   Philip Jones, *Art & Life: The Memoir of a Man Bearing Witness to the Remarkable World of Heide*, (Sydney: Allen & Unwin, 2004), p. 200.

8   Editorial, *Herald*, 23 February 1940.

9   Pat Jarrett, 'Allen', papers of Lord and Lady Casey MS12565, 3413/1 State Library Victoria.

10 'Designing Fabrics', *Australian Woman's World*, June (1940), p. 24.

11 *The Daily News*, 9 September 1941.

12 Diane Langmore, 'Casey, Lady Ethel Marian (Maie)' *Australian Dictionary of Biography*, (Melbourne: Melbourne University Press, 2007), 17.

13 Roger Butler note to John McPhee, archives and manuscripts MS 42, Box 1, Frances Burke (Artist File), Research Library, National Gallery of Australia.

14 Talks Department, *Design in Everyday Things*, Australian Broadcasting Commission, 1941, p. 3.

15 Michael Bogle, *Design in Australia 1880–1970* (Sydney: Craftsman House, 1998), p. 105.

16 Bernard Kearns, *The Story of the Melbourne Little Theatre 1931–1950* (Melbourne: The Melbourne Little Theatre, 1950).

17 Editorial, *Herald*, 7 September 1946.

18 Editorial, *Age*, 24 November 1951.

19 Frank Thring scrapbook, Performing Arts Museum (Melbourne: Melbourne Little Theatre South Yarra), p. 78, referenced by Peter Fitzpatrick, *The Two Frank Thrings* (Melbourne: Monash University Publishing, 2012), p. 334.

20 JWK was the theatre critic James W Kern. *Port Philip Gazette*, 1,1 (1952), p. 33.

21 Peter Fitzpatrick, *The Two Frank Thrings* (Melbourne: Monash University Publishing, 2012), p. 334.

22 Editorial, 'Arrow Closes—It Won't Stage Froth,' *Argus*, 16 September 1953.

23 Editorial, 'Life Made Easy for the Housewife', *Advocate* (Burnie), 24 September 1947.

24 Editorial, 'US Industrialists Watch Women's Tastes', *Argus*, 22 October 1947.

25 Editorial, 'Designer's Trip to be Refreshed', *Age*, 26 July 1949.

26 Editorial, 'Industrial Designer Returns', *Daily Telegraph* (Sydney), 20 January 1949.

27 Editorial, 'They Look on Us as Drudges', *Argus*, 25 January 1951.

28 ibid.

29 Editorial, 'Industrial Designer is Home Again', *Sunday Herald* (Sydney), 18 September 1949.

30 Editorial, 'Color May Make You Morning Happy', *Age*, 22 March 1950.

31 Editorial, 'Roundabout', *Argus*, 22 March 1950.

32 Editorial, 'Oversea [sic] Furnishings Trend to Simplicity', *Age*, 21 August 1953.

33 Frances Burke, 'untitled', handwritten notes for talk, 1953, held by the National Gallery of Victoria.

34 Frances Burke, 'Modern Furnishing Fabrics', *Architecture and Arts*, November 1954, pp. 30–1.

35 Frances Burke, 'Choose Furnishings With Care', *New Country Crafts*, 5, 7 (1956), pp. 20–1.

36 Jan Meredith, 'Soft Furnishing Secrets', *Australian Home Beautiful*, 28, 8 (1949), p. 39.

37 Editorial, 'Local Designer Adopts "Unit Colour" Theme', *Australian Home Beautiful*, 37, 11 (1958), p. 36.

38 Anne Purves, interview by Robyn Oswald-Jacobs, 19 April 1994.

5 ARCHITECTURAL COLLABORATIONS AND COMMISSIONS

1   Robin Boyd, 'The Artists Embark', *Lines: The Annual Journal of the Architectural Students' Society of the Royal Victorian Institute of Architects*, 1939, pp. 12–13.

2   Denise Whitehouse, *Design for Life: Grant and Mary Featherston* (Melbourne: Heide Museum of Modern Art, 2018), p. 12.

3   Editorial, *Argus*, 21 December 1939.

4   *Smudges*, journal of the RVIA Students' Society, 2, 10, (1940).

5   Rebecca Hawcroft, 'The Lucky Escapees: European Architects in Postwar Sydney' in *The Other Moderns: Sydney's Forgotten European Design Legacy*, ed. Rebecca Hawcroft (Sydney: NewSouth, 2017), p. 54.

6   Molly Grey, 'Wartime Furnishing in Australia', *Australia: National Journal*, June–August (1940), p. 64.

7   Editorial, 'Modern Décor in New Beauty Salon', *The Sun* (Sydney), 7 February 1940, p. 18.

8   Neil Clerehan, 'Roy Grounds', *Architecture*, January–March (1954–5), pp. 22–3.

9   Frances Burke, Pioneering Design, lecture to the East Melbourne Historical Society (transcript), 21 April 1980.

10 The *Rangga* design appears to be a representation of waterholes or campfires and the tracks between them. Burke read the work of W Baldwin Spencer who lived and travelled in the Central and Western Desert areas, where the word 'rangga' is used to describe a sacred object.

11 Genevieve Lansell, interview by Robyn Oswald-Jacobs, 25 January 2020. Sir Reginald Ansett purchased Moondah in Mount Eliza, on Victoria's Mornington Peninsula, in 1947, and began restoring and refreshing the building, with the fit-out including Burke fabrics in every room. The site re-opened as the Hotel Manyung, a five-star luxury hotel, 'Where your holiday dreams are waiting to come true', was sold by Ansett in 1957. www.mpnews.com.au, 5 July 2016.

12 Ann Imrie, ed., *1952–1980 Architecture of Guilford Bell* (South Melbourne: Proteus,1982), pp. 13–15.

13 Graham Fisher, cited in Leon Van Schaik, ed., *Bell: The Life and Work of Guilford Bell 1912–1992* (Melbourne: Schwartz City, 1999), p. 14.

14 Frances Burke, Pioneering Design, lecture to the East Melbourne Historical Society (transcript), 21 April 1980.

15 Gordon Shebly, photocopy typewritten diary, 1949–53, RMIT Design Archives, 0070/2012 Box 2.

16 Philip Goad in *Bell: The Life and Work of Guilford Bell 1912–1992*, ed. Leon Van Schaik (Melbourne: Schwartz City, 1999), p. 113.

17 Robin Boyd, 'House of Tomorrow', (Small Homes Section), *Age*, 12 October 1949.

18 Burke quoted in Felicity St John Moore, exhibition catalogue, *Classical Modernism: The George Bell Circle* (National Gallery Victoria, 1992), p. 92.

19 Frances Burke, taken from twelve interviews by Robyn Oswald-Jacobs, February 1991 – February 1992.

20 ibid.

21 Julie Willis, 'The Health of Modernism' in *Australian Modern: The Architecture of Stephenson & Turner*, ed. Philip Goad et al. (Melbourne: Melbourne University Publishing, 2004), p. 29.

22 ibid.

23 Margaret Lawrence, press release, Australian Textile Designers Work on a Large Scale: Striking Designs by Frances Burke, 1952.

24 Editorial, *Age* ,14 April 1951.

25 Philip Goad and David Nichols, 'Early Learning: The Modern Kindergarten' in *Community: Building Modern Australia*, eds Hannah Lewi & David Nichols (Sydney: University of New South Wales Press, 2010), p. 71.

26 Robin Boyd, *Victorian Modern: 111 Years of Modern Architecture in Victoria* (Melbourne: Architectural Students' Society of the Royal Victorian Institute of Architects, 1947), p. 57.

27 'Miss Smith Street 1950', *Smith Street Traders Association*, 1950, p. 7.

28 Editorial, 'New Kindergarten Opened at Fitzroy', *Age*, 31 March 1950.

29 Editorial, 'Modern Maternal Centre', *Age*, 30 November 1951.

30 Editorial, 'Critical of Furnishings', *News Adelaide*, 26 March 1952.
31 Editorial, 'Crusader for Modern Color', *People*, 25 September 1952, p. 18.
32 ibid.
33 James Anderson, History of Lake Eildon, www.lakeeildon.com/hist, 16 August 2019.
34 Heritage Victoria, 2007–08 Survey of Post-War Built Heritage in Victoria, (040-025), p. 276.
35 Editorial, *Architecture and Arts* June, (1965), pp. 36–7.
36 Rod Buchanan, 'The Secret Life of the Professor', Melbourne School of Psychological Sciences, University of Melbourne, https://pursuit.unimelb.edu.au/articles/the-secret-life-of-the-professor; October 2016.
37 Fabie Chamberlin, interview by Robyn Oswald-Jacobs, 16 March 1995.
38 Frances Burke, Pioneering Design, lecture to the East Melbourne Historical Society, (transcript), 21 April 1980.
39 Virginia Rigney, CCCT—Frances Burke Publication, email, 23 April 2020.
40 ibid.
41 Doreen Hungerford, 'Dazzling First Night at Theatre', *Canberra Times*, 25 June 1965.
42 Virginia Rigney, CCCT—Frances Burke Publication, email, 23 April 2020.
43 Editorial, *News Adelaide*, 26 March 1952.
44 Robin Boyd, 'Out of the Forest Primeval', *Lines: A Journal of Architecture and Allied Interests*, (1940–41), p. 22.
45 Margaret Preston, 'Applications of Aboriginal Design', *Art in Australia*, 3, 31 (1930), p. 51.
46 Margaret Lawrence, 'Aboriginal Art Has Inspired Australian Design', *Pacific Neighbours*, 4, 1 (1949), pp. 46–50.

6 THE AUSTRALIAN POSTWAR HOME

1 Philip Goad, 'Featherston Chairs: Microcosms of Melbourne Design 1947–1974', *Transition*, Winter (1988), p. 90.
2 Neil Clerehan, preface, *Featherston Chairs* (Melbourne: National Gallery of Victoria, 1988), p. 7.
3 Phyllis Murphy, interview by Robyn Oswald-Jacobs and Nanette Carter, 17 September 2019.
4 Peter McIntyre, interview by Robyn Oswald-Jacobs and Nanette Carter, 4 September 2019.
5 Lesley Stahle, 'Outlook for Moderns', *Australian House and Garden*, 30, 10, (1951), p. 53.
6 Joan Leyser, *Sydney Morning Herald*, 17 December 1953.
7 ibid.
8 W. Scott, 'Through Toil to Beauty', *Australian Home Beautiful*, 32, 8 (1953), p. 29.
9 Philip Goad, 'Foreword' in *Beaumaris Modern: Modernist Houses in Beaumaris*, ed. Fiona Austin (Melbourne: Melbourne Books, 2018), pp. 8–9.
10 Alma Somers, 'Accent on Style', *Australian House and Garden*, May (1955), p. 16.
11 ibid.
12 Lewis Springfield, 'Sunshine Homes', *South-West Pacific*, 30 (1953), pp. 60–2.
13 Editorial, 'Renovated Old Home', *Sun-Herald*, 4 April 1954.
14 Howard Tanner, Beryl Guertner, *Australian Dictionary of Biography*, 17 (Melbourne: Melbourne University Press, 2007).
15 Karl Langer, *Sub-tropical Housing* (Brisbane: University of Queensland, 1944).
16 Robin Boyd, *Australia's Home* (Melbourne: Melbourne University Press, 1952), p. 150.
17 Editorial, *Australian House and Garden*, October (1957), pp. 16–17, 64–5.
18 Frank Colin Hassell, https://www.architectsdatabase.unisa.edu.au/arch_full.asp?Arch_ID=23.
19 Maryam Gusheh & Catherine Lassen, 'Informal Modern Holiday Houses' in *Leisure Space: The Transformation of Sydney 1945–1970*, eds Paul Hogben & Judith O'Callaghan (Sydney, NewSouth, 2014), p. 224.
20 Editorial, 'No Koalas Please', *Age*, 5 April 1967.

7. A LIFE BY DESIGN

1 Colin Barrie, dean of Faculty of Art RMIT, speech on conferral honorary doctorate for Frances Burke 1987, RMIT Design Archives.
2 Frances Burke, acceptance speech on conferral honorary doctorate, RMIT Faculty of Art, 1987, RMIT Design Archives.
3 Frances Burke, keynote speech RMIT Faculty of Art Graduation ceremony, 1987, RMIT Design Archives.
4 'Two Year Plan for Living', see illustrations and transcript in Chapter 2.
5 Burke quoted in Bob Quirk, 'Tribal Motifs Go Around the World', *Australasian Post*, 24 January 1952, p. 17.

HOUSEWIFE HOME AND FAMILY

6ᴰ MONTHLY

OCTOBER, 1960

MISS FRANCES BURKE
Brilliant Australian
Textile Designer

Select bibliography

Alcorso, Claudio, *The Wind You Say* (Sydney: Angus & Robertson), 1993.

Ambrus, Caroline, *Australian Women Artists: First Fleet to 1945: History, Hearsay and Her Say* (Woden, ACT: Irrepressible Press), 1992.

Austin, Fiona, et. al., *Beaumaris Modern: Modernist Houses in Beaumaris*, (Melbourne: Melbourne Books), 2018.

Bogle, Michael, *Design in Australia 1880–1970* (Sydney: Craftsman House, G+B Arts International), 1998.

Bomford, Jeanette, *Circles of Friendship: The Centenary History of the Lyceum Club* (Melbourne: Australian Scholarly Publishing), 2012.

Boyd, Robin, *Victorian Modern, 111 years of Modern Architecture in Victoria* (Melbourne: Architectural Students' Society of the Royal Victorian Institute of Architects), 1947.

Carter, Nanette, *Savage Luxury: Modernist Design in Melbourne* (Melbourne: Heide Museum of Modern Art), 2007.

Casey, Maie, *Tides and Eddies* (United Kingdom: Joseph), 1966.

Eagle, Mary and Minchin, Jan, *The George Bell School: Students, Friends, Influences* (Melbourne & Sydney: Deutscher Art Publications & Resolution Press), 1981.

Edquist, Harriet, *Michael O'Connell: The Lost Modernist* (Melbourne: Melbourne Books), 2011.

Goad, Philip, Rowan Wilken and Julie Willis, *Australian Modern: The Architecture of Stephenson & Turner* (Melbourne: Miegunyah Press), 2004.

Hawcroft, Rebecca, *The Other Moderns: Sydney's Forgotten European Design Legacy* (Sydney: NewSouth Publishing), 2017.

Helmer, June, *George Bell: The Art of Influence* (Melbourne: Greenhouse Publications), 1985.

Isaac, Geoff, *Featherston* (Sydney: Thames and Hudson), 2017.

Jones, Philip, *Art & Life: The Memoir of a Man Bearing Witness to the Remarkable World of Heide* (Sydney: Allen & Unwin), 2004.

Langmore, Diane, *Glittering Surfaces: A Life of Maie Casey* (Sydney: Allen and Unwin), 1997.

Lewi, Hannah and Philip Goad *Australia Modern: Architecture, Landscape and Design 1925–1975* (Melbourne: Thames and Hudson), 2019.

Lewi, Hannah and David Nicholls (eds), *Community: Building Modern Australia* (Sydney: UNSW Press), 2010.

Lord, Margaret, *Interior Decoration: A Guide to Furnishing the Australian Home* (Sydney: Ure Smith), 1944.

McPhee, John, *Australian Decorative Arts in The Australian National Gallery* (Canberra: Australian National Gallery), 1988.

Peers, Juliette, *More Than Just Gumtrees: A Personal, Social and Artistic History of the Melbourne Society of Women Painters and Sculptors* (Melbourne: The Society in association with Dawn Revival Press), 1993.

Richards, Michaela, *The Best Style, Marion Hall Best and Australian Interior Design 1935–1975* (Sydney: Art & Australia Books, an imprint of G+B Arts International Limited), 1993.

Serle, Geoffrey, *Robin Boyd: A Life*, (Melbourne: Melbourne University Press), 1995.

St John Moore, Felicity, *Classical Modernism: The George Bell Circle* (Melbourne: National Gallery of Victoria), 1992.

Stephen, Ann, Philip Goad and Andrew McNamara (eds), *Modern Times: The Untold Story of Modernism in Australia* (Melbourne: Miegunyah), 2008.

Van Schaik, Leon (ed.), *Bell: The Life and Work of Guilford Bell 1912–1992* (Melbourne: Bookman Press), 1999.

Whitehouse, Denise, *Design for Life: Grant and Mary Featherston* (Melbourne: Heide Museum of Modern Art), 2018.

Zilles, Lauretta, *Buda and the Leviny Family* (Buda Historic Home and Garden), 2010.

Copyright, permissions and image credits

Copyright in the works of Frances Burke is owned by RMIT University and provided courtesy of RMIT Design Archives.

Every effort has been made to contact persons owning copyright of the images reproduced in this book.

ABBREVIATIONS

MAAS   Museum of Applied Arts and Sciences, Sydney
NGA   National Gallery of Australia
NGV   National Gallery of Victoria
RMIT   RMIT University
SLM   Sydney Living Museums
SLV   State Library Victoria

COVER

Tiger Stripe, photographer: John Gollings, RMIT Design Archives, © RMIT University.

PRELIMINARY PAGES

ii *The Age*, Fairfax; iii Frances Burke signature, photographer: David Campbell, RMIT Design Archives, © RMIT University; vi Small Homes Service of the Royal Victorian Institute of Architects & 'The Age', 1953. *Costs & Quantities of a Modern Home.* Jack Cheesman collection, Architecture Museum, University of South Australia, © RMIT University; ix Goad Family Collection.

1 FINDING HER WAY

x-1 *Canna Leaf* (c. 1940) Frances Burke (designer), Burway Prints, Melbourne (manufacturer), screenprinted cotton, NGV, Melbourne. Presented by Dr Frances Burke 1989, © RMIT University; 2 Frances Burke Collection, RMIT Design Archives, © RMIT University; 3 Private Collection, © RMIT University; 4 Coburg Historical Society; 5 Melbourne University Archives, *St Paul's Cathedral spire under construction*, photographer: Sir Russell Grimwade; 6 *Homeopathic Hospital*, Melbourne, J D Meade postcard collection, SLV; 7 Frances Burke Collection, RMIT Design Archives, © RMIT University; 8 Phyl Waterhouse, Alannah Coleman and Charles Bush, *Argus* photographer 1935, SLV, State Library of Victoria Foundation gift, 2000; 9 Collection of Janet (Bardin) Robinson; 10 above Collection of Janet (Bardin) Robinson; 10 below Exterior View of the School of Applied Art (MTC), cnr La Trobe & Bowen Sts, Melbourne c. 1920–30, James Alexander Smith Collection, SLV; 11 Courtesy Private Collection, photographer: John Gollings, © RMIT University; 12 James Quinn (Australia; England; France, b. 1871, d. 1951) *George Bell (artist and critic)* (1940), oil on canvas, 92.1 × 71.1 cm, Art Gallery of New South Wales, purchased 1940. Photo: Brenton McGeachie; 13 Collection of Janet (Bardin) Robinson; 14 left Michael O'Connell *Bacchante*: Curtain length c. 1934, linoleum block printing on linen, National Gallery of Australia, Canberra, 1980. © Michael O'Connell/DACS, Copyright Agency 2021; 14 right *Table Talk*, 8 July 1937; 16 Caroline Simpson Library & Research Collection, SLM, © RMIT University; 18 Frances Burke Collection, RMIT Design Archives, © RMIT University; 19 MAAS, Gift of Frances Burke under the Australian Government Taxation Incentives for the Arts Scheme, 1985. Photo Kate Chidlow, © RMIT University; 20 Screenprint on cotton, 96 × 72.6 cm, NGA, Canberra, Gift of Frances Burke 1984, © RMIT University; 21 Courtesy of Ararat Gallery TAMA, Ararat Rural City Council and MDP, Photography & Video, © RMIT University; 22 Frances Burke Collection, RMIT Design Archives, © RMIT University; 23 Courtesy of Ararat Gallery TAMA, Ararat Rural City Council and MDP Photography & Video, © RMIT University.

2 FORGING A CAREER IN DESIGN

24-5 *Tapa Cloth* (c. 1938) Frances Burke (designer) Burway Prints, dress fabric c. 1938 Screenprint on cotton 54 × 89 cm, NGA, Canberra, Gift of Frances Burke 1982, © RMIT University; 26 Print, Australia, 1901–1910: Spencer and Gillen Collection, Museum Victoria; 27 *View of Industrial and Technological Museum from corner of Swanston St & LaTrobe St, Melbourne*, c. 1930s; SMV Negatives, Museum History Collection, Museum Victoria; 28 Photographer: Sutcliffe Pty Ltd, Laurie Carew Collection, RMIT Design Archives, © RMIT University; 29 *Table Talk*, 1 February 1934, SLV; 30-1 Frances Burke Collection, RMIT Design Archives, © RMIT University; 32 above Public Records Office

Victoria, VPRS 12343/P/0001 Unit 10, Box 14 Business Registration Card Number 67899 for Burway Prints; 32 below *Burway Print* 1939, screenprint matrix, 18 × 40 cm, NGA, Canberra, Gift of Frances Burke 1986, © RMIT University; 33 Photographer: John Gollings; 34 above left Screenprint on linen, 102 × 43 cm, NGA, Canberra, Gift of Frances Burke 1982, © RMIT University; 34 above middle Screenprint on paper, 180 × 288 cm, NGA, Canberra, Gift of Frances Burke 1986, © RMIT University; 34 above right *Bouquet* (1940) Fabric piece, screenprinted, Frances Burke Fabrics Pty Ltd, Victoria, Australia. Gift of Frances Burke under the Australian Government Taxation Incentives for the Arts Scheme 1985, MAAS, © RMIT University; 34 below Photographer: Ralph Illedge, Frances Burke Collection, RMIT Design Archives, © RMIT University; 35 *The Age*, Fairfax; 36 Illustrator unknown, Georges Archive, MA Thesis 1997, Robyn Oswald-Jacobs; 37-40 *Australian Woman's Day*, 13 February 1950, SLV; 41 Frances Burke Collection, RMIT Design Archives, © RMIT University; 42-3 Cotton, paper, card and collotape 57.5 × 43.5 cm, NGA, Canberra, Gift of Frances Burke 1987, © RMIT University; 44 Box 1504, Coles-Myer Archive, SLV; 45 *The Herald*, Tuesday 10 January 1939, SLV; 46 above Box 1809, Coles-Myer Archive, SLV; 46 below *The Home*, March 1937, SLV; 47 Illustrator unknown, *Georges Gazette*, Georges Archive, MA Thesis 1997, Robyn Oswald-Jacobs; 48 Screenprint on cotton, 108 × 87 cm, NGA, Canberra, Gift of Frances Burke 1982, © RMIT University; 50 Frances Burke Collection, RMIT Design Archives, © RMIT University; 51-3 Courtesy of Ararat Gallery TAMA, Ararat Rural City Council and MDP Photography & Video, © RMIT University.

3 DEVELOPING A NATIONAL MARKET

54-5 *Tiger Stripe* (1938) Frances Burke Collection, RMIT Design Archives, © RMIT University; 56 Photographer: Lyle Fowler, Commercial Photographic Co., Harold Paynting Collection, SLV; 57 Melbourne University Archives, Myer Emporium, 1979.0180, unit 191; 58 Frederick McCarthy, *Australian Aboriginal Art*, Australian Museum Sydney, 1956, SLV; 59 left Boans advertisement, *The Daily News*, Perth, 9/9/1941, SLWA; 59 middle Coplands advertisement, *Daily Advertiser*, Wagga Wagga, 16/9/53, SLNSW; 59 right above Trittons advertisement, *The Courier-Mail*, Brisbane, 23/10/1941 SLQ; 59 right below Frank Griff advertisement, *Barrier Daily Truth*, 24/9/54, SLNSW; 60 *Architecture and Arts*, April 1954, SLV; 61 John Warlow, Frances Burke Collection, RMIT Design Archives, © RMIT University; 62 Keith Winser, *Furnishing the Australian Home: A Complete Guide for Every Budget*, Motor Manual Publications, 1954, SLV; 63 Bauer Media Pty Limited, *Australian House and Garden*, April 1953, SLV; 64 above Bauer Media Pty Limited, *Australian Home Beautiful* July 1954, SLV; 64 below *Architecture and Arts*, September 1952, SLV; 65 *Architecture and Arts*, November 1954, SLV; 66 Bauer Media Pty Limited, *Australian Home Beautiful*, July 1954, SLV; 67 Bauer Media Pty Limited, *Australian Home Beautiful*, October 1963, SLV; 68 Bauer Media Pty Limited, *Australian Home Beautiful*, November 1955. Collection Dean Keep & Jeromie Maver. © Bill Onus/Copyright Agency, 2020; 70 above Curtain [Native Theme] c. 1930, lino block on linen, 211 × 91.5 cm, photographer: Tim Wheeler. Gift of Tanya Crothers & Darani Lewers, 1979, Penrith Regional Gallery, Home of the Lewers Bequest Collection; 70 below Modernage Fabrics, Silk and Textile Printers Ltd, Sydney and Hobart manufacturer Margaret Preston (designer) *Adina, fabric length* 1947 screenprinted rayon 99 × 86 cm, NGV, Gift of Professor Sir Joseph Burke, 1979 (D75C-1979) © Margaret Preston/Copyright Agency, 2020; 71 Annan Fabrics, Caroline Simpson Library & Research Collection, Sydney Living Museums. Gift of the Morris family; 72 *Australian National Journal*, June–Aug 1940, SLV; 73 Margaret Lord, *Interior Decoration: A Guide to Furnishing the Australian Home*, Ure Smith Pty. Ltd. Sydney,1944; 74 Photographer: Sutcliffe Pty Ltd, Frederick Sterne Collection, RMIT Design Archives, © RMIT University; 75-6 *Papers of Marion Hall Best 1935–1970* MS 31 NGA Research Library & Archives; 77 Caroline Simpson Library & Research Collection, SLM. Photo © Antonia Blaxland; 78 *British Vogue* Spring Summer 1956 Australian Supplement p.60, SLV. © Helmut Newton/ADAGP. Copyright Agency 2020; 79 News Ltd/Newspix; 80 left Collection of Caroline Hooper; 80 right–81 right Collection of Beverley Ednie; 82 Caroline Simpson Library & Research Collection, SLM, © RMIT University; 84 Screenprint on cotton 109 × 90 cm, NGA, Canberra, Gift of Frances Burke 1986, © RMIT University; 85 Screenprint on cotton 95.5 × 90 cm, NGA, Canberra, Gift of Frances Burke 1986, © RMIT University; 86 Screenprint on paper, 248 × 368 cm, NGA, Canberra, Gift of Frances Burke 1987, © RMIT University; 87 Caroline Simpson Library & Research Collection, SLM, © RMIT University.

4 CREATING THE FRANCES BURKE BRAND

88-9 *Fern* (c. 1940) screenprinted cotton 46 × 90.2 cm, NGV, presented by Dr Frances Burke, 1989, © RMIT University; 90 above Collection of Janet (Bardin) Robinson;

90 below Screenprint on cotton, 76 × 87 cm, NGA, Canberra. Gift of Frances Burke 1982, © RMIT University; **91** Bauer Media Pty Limited, *Australian House and Garden*, December 1949, SLV; **92 in descending order** *Totem* selvedge, Caroline Simpson Library and Research Collection, SLM, © RMIT University; *Tiger Stripe* selvedge, Courtesy of Ararat Gallery TAMA, Ararat Rural City Council and MDP Photography and Video, © RMIT University; *Rangga* selvedge, Caroline Simpson Library and Research Collection, SLM. © RMIT University; *Staccato* selvedge, Caroline Simpson Library and Research Collection, SLM, © RMIT University; **94** Papers of Frances Burke c. 1940s–c. 1960s, MS 42, NGA Research Library & Archives, © RMIT University; **95** Frances Burke Collection, RMIT Design Archives, © RMIT University; **96 letter** Oil on cardboard mounted on a wooden frame each 183 × 60 × 2.5 cm, NGA, Canberra, Gift of the Lady Casey; **96 swatch** Screenprinted cotton 46 × 90.2 cm, NGV, presented by Dr Frances Burke 1989, © RMIT University; **97** MS 1840/Series 8/File 13 (Box 33) National Library of Australia; **98** Australian Broadcasting Commission, *Booklet Design in Everyday Things*, ABC, 1941, SLV; **99** *The Age*, 24 November 1951, SLV; **100–1** Performing Arts Museum Collection, Melbourne; **102** Collection of Janet (Bardin) Robinson; **103** Berenice Harris Collection, RMIT Design Archives, © RMIT University; **104 left** Bauer Media Pty Limited, *Australian Home Beautiful*, July 1949, SLV; **104 right** Bauer Media Pty Limited, *Australian Home Beautiful*, December 1958, SLV; **105** *The New Australian Post*, 6 November 1952, SLV; **106** Collection of Janet (Bardin) Robinson; **107 above** Papers of Frances Burke c. 1940s–1960s MS 42, NGA Research Library & Archives, © RMIT University; **107 below** Frances Burke Collection, Courtesy RMIT Design Archives, © RMIT University; **109** Bauer Media Pty Limited, *Australian Home Beautiful*, October 1955, SLV; **110** Bauer Media Pty Limited, *Australian Home Beautiful*, August 1949, SLV; **111 above** Caroline Simpson Library & Research Collection, SLM, © RMIT University; **111 below** Screenprint on paper with pastel additions 49 × 99 cm, NGA, Canberra, Gift of Frances Burke 1986, © RMIT University; **112** Frances Burke Collection, RMIT Design Archives, © RMIT University; **114–15** MAAS, Gift of Frances Burke under the Australian Government Taxation Incentives for the Arts Scheme 1985, © RMIT University; **116** Screenprint 87 × 91 cm, NGA, Canberra, Gift of Frances Burke 1984, © RMIT University; **117** Courtesy of Ararat Gallery TAMA, Ararat Rural City Council and MDP Photography & Video, © RMIT University.

5 ARCHITECTURAL COLLABORATIONS AND COMMISSIONS

118–19 *Bal* (1945–51) Caroline Simpson Library & Research Collection, SLM, © RMIT University; **120** *Architecture: Journal of the RAIA*, January 1950 cover, SLV; **121** Special Collection, Architecture Building and Planning Library, University of Melbourne; **122 above** Photographer: Sutcliffe Pty Ltd, 1939–1945, SLV; **122 below** Screenprint on linen 115 × 90.5 cm, NGA, Canberra, Gift of Frances Burke 1982, © RMIT University; **123** *Smudges: journal of the RVIA Students' Society* v.2 no.10, January 1940, Architecture Building and Planning Library, University of Melbourne; **124** MAAS, Gift of Frances Burke under the Australian Government Taxation Incentives for the Arts Scheme 1985, © RMIT University; **125–6** Commercial Photography Co, H2004.65/34, SLV; **127 above** *The Home*, March 1942, SLV; **127 below** Caroline Simpson Library & Research Collection, SLM, © RMIT University; **128** *Walkabout*, November 1954, SLV; **129 above** Courtesy of the Guilford Bell Archive; **129 below** Courtesy of Ararat Gallery TAMA, Ararat Rural City Council and MDP Photography & Video, © RMIT University; **130** MAAS, Gift of Frances Burke under the Australian Government Taxation Incentives for the Arts Scheme 1985, © RMIT University; **131 above** Screenprinted cotton 91 × 82 cm, NGV, presented by Dr Frances Burke 1989, © RMIT University; **131 below** Courtesy Southern Cross Ski Club Lodge, Mt Buller, Victoria; **132** Exhibition at Melbourne Exhibition Buildings, 1949, photographer: Wolfgang Sievers, Wolfgang Sievers photographic archive, © National Library of Australia; **133 above left** B H Brindley (ed.), *Practical Household Painting*, Colorgravure, Melbourne, n.d; **133 above right** Screenprinted cotton 64.5 × 45 cm, NGV, Melbourne presented by Dr Frances Burke 1989, © RMIT University; **133 below** Caroline Simpson Library & Research Collection, SLM, © RMIT University; **134** Private Collection, photographer: Peter McIntyre; **135 above and below** Shaw Library, NGV; **135 below left** Frances Burke Collection, RMIT Design Archives, © RMIT University; **136** Photographer: Edwin G Adamson, SLV; **137 above** Photographer: Ingerson and Arnold Studios, Stephenson & Turner Archive, SLV; **137 below** Caroline Simpson Library & Research Collection, SLM, © RMIT University; **138 above** Photographer: Commercial Photographic Company, Stephenson & Turner Archive, SLV; **138 below** 86th Annual Report 30.6.1956, archive of The Alfred Hospital; **139** Archive of the Peter MacCallum Clinic; **140 above** Joan Waters, *The Lady Gowrie Child Centre: The Place, the People, the Program 1939-1999*, The Lady Gowrie Child Centre, 2000, SLV; **140 below** Screenprinted cotton 87.5 × 61.6 cm, NGV, presented by Dr Frances Burke 1989, © RMIT University; **141 above** Canberra Mothercraft Society Records, HMSS0043, Courtesy ACT Heritage Library; **141 below** *The Baby Health Centre, Yallourn, December 1949*: State Electricity Commission of Victoria Collection, Museum Victoria; **142–3** Travancore Archive; **143** Frances Burke Collection, RMIT Design Archives, © RMIT University; **144** Private collection; **145** Melbourne University Archives, Records of Yuncken Freeman Architects Pty Ltd and Predecessors photographs, 2018.0115.00632, *Eildon Theatre*, 1951 (Bates, Smart, McCutcheon architects); **146 above** Dr Ernest Fooks, photographer: Mark Strizic, SLV; **146 below** Screenprint on linen 56 × 125 cm, NGA,

Canberra, gift of Frances Burke 1984, © RMIT University; **147** *Architecture and Arts* March 1957, SLV; **148 above** Collection of Harry Ernest; **148 below** MAAS, Gift of Frances Burke under the Australian Government Taxation Incentives for the Arts Scheme 1985, © RMIT University; **149** Melbourne University Archives, *Oscar Oeser, Child Study Centre*, University of Melbourne Department of Psychology, 1981; **151** National Archives of Australia: Trade Publicity Branch; B942/2; States–ACT, Canberra 1964; **152 above** Screenprinted cotton 300 × 122.3 cm, NGV, Melbourne presented by Dr Frances Burke 1989, © RMIT University; **152 below** Screenprint on linen 1964, Canberra Theatre Centre, Civic Square Canberra, © RMIT University; **153** Auditorium of the Canberra Theatre Centre 1966, Canberra Theatre Trust Collection, 007256, ACT Heritage Library; **154** Photographer: Leone Mills, 1965, SLV; **155–6** Caroline Simpson Library & Research Collection, SLM, © RMIT University; **159** Courtesy of Ararat Gallery TAMA, Ararat Rural City Council and MDP Photography & Video, © RMIT University; **160** Screenprint on linen 45.5 × 95 cm, NGA, Canberra, Gift of Frances Burke 1986, © Copyright RMIT; **161** Courtesy of Ararat Gallery TAMA, Ararat Rural City Council and MDP Photography & Video, © RMIT University.

6 THE AUSTRALIAN POSTWAR HOME

162–3 *Staccato* (1962) Courtesy of Ararat Gallery TAMA, Ararat Rural City Council and MDP Photography & Video, © RMIT University; **164** Bauer Media Pty Limited, *Australian Home Beautiful*, April 1954, Design Special Collection, Swinburne University Library; **166** Collection of Phyllis Murphy; **167 above** Frances Burke Collection, RMIT Design Archives, © RMIT University; **167 below** Collection of Phyllis Murphy; **168** Bauer Media Pty Limited, *Australian House and Garden*, August 1953, State Library of New South Wales; **169 above** Ashton House Mornington, designed by Roy Grounds, photographer: Lyle Fowler, 1951, SLV; **169 below** Screenprinted cotton 89.7 × 94.2 cm NGV, Melbourne presented by Dr Frances Burke 1989 (CT63-1989) © RMIT University; **170** Collection of Laura Jocic, © RMIT University; **170–1** Photographer: Lyle Fowler c. 1953, SLV; **172** Bauer Media Pty Limited, *Australian Home Beautiful*, April 1953, SLV; **173** Bauer Media Pty Limited, *Australian Home Beautiful*, January 1953, SLV; **174** Bauer Media Pty Limited, *Australian House and Garden*, July 1953, collection Alison Alexander; **175** Courtesy of Ararat Gallery TAMA, Ararat Rural City Council and MDP Photography & Video, © RMIT University; **176 above** Bauer Media Pty Limited, *Australian House and Garden*, May 1955, SLV; **176 below** Collection Alison Alexander; **177** Bauer Media Pty Limited, *Australian House and Garden*, July 1966, SLV; **178–9** Collection of Keith and Christian Macdonald, photographer: John Gollings; **180** *South West Pacific*, Issue 30, SLV; **181 above** Screenprint on cotton 130 × 87 cm, NGA, Canberra, Gift of Frances Burke 1984, © RMIT University; **181 below** Bauer Media Pty Limited, *Australian Homemaker*, June 1957, Special Collections, Deakin University Library; **182** Bauer Media Pty Limited, *Australian House and Garden*, January 1954, SLV; **183 left** Bauer Media Pty Limited, *Australian House and Garden*, September 1955, SLV; **183 right** Bauer Media Pty Limited, *Australian Home Beautiful*, February 1955, SLV; **184** Bauer Media Pty Limited, *Australian Home Beautiful*, April 1956, SLV; **185** Bauer Media Pty Limited, *Australian House and Garden*, August 1955, SLV, © Ian Mckenzie/Copyright Agency, 2020; **186** Bauer Media Pty Limited, *Australian Home Beautiful*, April 1955, SLV; **187** Courtesy of the Smith Family; **188** MAAS, Gift of Frances Burke under the Australian Government Taxation Incentives for the Arts Scheme 1985, © RMIT University; **190** Courtesy of Ararat Gallery TAMA, Ararat Rural City Council and MDP Photography & Video, © Copyright RMIT; **191** Caroline Simpson Library & Research Collection, SLM, © RMIT University; **192** MAAS, Gift of Frances Burke under the Australian Government Taxation Incentives for the Arts Scheme 1985, © RMIT University; **193** Courtesy of Ararat Gallery TAMA, Ararat Rural City Council and MDP Photography & Video, © RMIT University.

7 A LIFE BY DESIGN

194–5 *Mosaic* (1962) Courtesy of Ararat Gallery TAMA, Ararat Rural City Council and MDP Photography & Video, © RMIT University; **196 above** Private Collection, © RMIT University; **196 below** Frances Burke Collection, RMIT Design Archives, © RMIT University; **197** Private Collection, © Copyright RMIT; **198** Frances Burke Collection, RMIT Design Archives, © RMIT University; **199** *The Age*, Fairfax; **200–1** Installation view Elder Wing, Art Gallery of South Australia, Adelaide, photographer: Saul Steed; **201** NGA (1988), poster for *Australian Decorative Arts 1788–1988* exhibition, NGA Research Library Archive Collection, Canberra, © NGA; **203** Collection of Buda Historic Home and Garden, Castlemaine, photographer: Vivienne Hamilton.

ENDMATTER

204 Courtesy of Ararat Gallery TAMA, Ararat Rural City Council and MDP Photography & Video, © RMIT University; **206** Frances Burke Collection, RMIT Design Archives, © RMIT University; **210** *Housewife, Home and Family*, Progressive Housewives Association of Victoria (defunct 1991), Melbourne, Frances Burke Collection, RMIT Design Archives; **214** Private Collection, photographer: John Gollings, © RMIT University.

Acknowledgements

We are delighted that the Miegunyah Fund chose to support the publication of this book.

This research project was generously funded by State Library Victoria and the University of Melbourne through the award of the Redmond Barry Fellowship, which enabled us to undertake broader and deeper research into Frances Burke's world. The Collections Management staff at both institutions were extremely helpful, in particular our liaison librarian Gerard Hayes at the State Library, and Susie Shears, Cultural Collections coordinator at the University of Melbourne. Sophie Garrett, reference archivist at the Melbourne University Archives, and staff at the Architecture Library in the Faculty of Architecture, Building and Planning, were consistently helpful and cheerful. Gail Schmidt kindly encouraged our queries and deftly managed the process for all the State Library's fellowship recipients.

We are indebted to Professor Philip Goad, Redmond Barry Distinguished Professor and chair of Architecture at the University of Melbourne, and Professor Alan Pert, director of the Melbourne School of Design of the University of Melbourne, for their advice and generous encouragement.

Thanks to Dr Lesley Harding, artistic director, and Kendrah Morgan, senior curator, from Heide Museum of Modern Art for their insights into the process of co-authoring and their enthusiastic support for a long overdue exhibition of Frances Burke's work.

Special thanks are due to Professor Cameron Bruhn, Dean and Head of School, School of Architecture, Universtiy of Queensland, for his insight into the potential contribution this research might make to the history of modernism in Australia and for championing its first stages.

Diane Masters (Romberg) was a crucial and continuing support to Frances Burke and Fabie Chamberlin, and was extremely generous in contributing information and understanding about their lives and work.

The authors wish to particularly acknowledge John McPhee, former curator of Australian Decorative Arts at the Australian National Gallery for his early recognition of Burke's importance to modern design in Australia and the timely acquisition of her work.

On behalf of their respective institutions, Grace Cochrane, AM, former senior curator of Australian Decorative Arts and Design, at the Powerhouse Museum (MAAS), and Terence Lane, former senior curator of Australian Art at the National Gallery of Victoria, are to be recognised for acquiring Burke's work.

The generous and timely assistance of Michael Lech, curator of the Caroline Simpson Library and Research Collection has been outstanding. Megan Martin, head of Collections and Access at Sydney Living Museums, also facilitated our experience of the institution's remarkable collection.

At the National Gallery of Victoria, Katie Somerville, senior curator Fashion and Textiles, Danielle Whitfield, senior curator Fashion and Textiles, and Luke Doyle in the Shaw Library were highly supportive of this research.

The team at the RMIT Design Archives have been diligent in continuing to collect, catalogue and make available the Frances Burke and other Australian design archives. In particular we thank Simone Rule, whose cheerful assistance and research advice was always appreciated.

The staff at the National Gallery of Australia, notably Rebecca Edwards, Syd and Fiona Myer Curator of Ceramics and Design, curatorial assistants Adam and Jessica, and librarian Vicki Marsh facilitated our access to its collections. Tracey Dall, manager, Publishing and Graphic Design, and Ellie Misios, rights and permissions officer, were extremely helpful.

We thank Virginia Rigney, senior curator of Visual Art at the Canberra Museum and Gallery, for her generous sharing of research into the Canberra Civic Centre and the Canberra Mothercraft Society, and for her continuing commitment to collaborative projects.

We are appreciative of the assistance of Jenny Lister, curator of Textiles and Fashion, at the Victoria & Albert Museum, London.

Julie Collins, curator at the Architecture Museum, UniSA, contributed useful suggestions.

Staff at the Museum of Applied Arts and Sciences, the Powerhouse Museum, were very helpful under difficult conditions.

At the Textile Art Museum Australia in Ararat, Astrid Krautschneider, curator, and subsequently Kate Davis, visual arts coordinator, were consistently interested in the project and helpful in making the collection available.

Claudia Funder, research service coordinator at the Arts Centre, Melbourne, gave us crucial assistance.

The librarians who worked to establish and continue to maintain the Design Special Collection at the Swinburne University of Technology Library have our thanks. Professor Scott Thompson-Whiteside is thanked for his support of Nanette Carter's research.

Many other people have contributed generously to the research for this book, they include: Alison Alexander, Michael Bogle, Alex Budd, Beverley Ednie, Graham Fisher, Chloe Fitzwilliams-Hyde, Peter Frawley, Jeanette Fry, Sarah Gillespie, Nola Hargreaves, Rebecca Hawcroft, Carole Hinchcliff, Caroline Hooper, Genevieve Lansell, Smaro Lazarakis, Christian Macdonald, Tom McEvoy, Marian Macgowan, Peter McIntyre, Phyllis Murphy, Poppy Nixon, Fiona Prossor, Catriona Quinn, Andrew Ray, Dan Robinson, Jon Robinson, Anna Sande, Michele Smith, Michelle Stillman, Yvonne von Hartel, Julie Willis and Lauretta Zilles.

Instagram followers have actively contributed through their interest, material they brought to our attention and the connections they kindly offered.

Jeromie Maver and Dean Keep generously contributed to the project as it evolved, with advice, information and encouragement.

Christopher Koller has been unfailingly cheerful while living with the disruption caused by this project.

Eminent photographer John Gollings provided generous support in time and in his outstanding photographic skills.

We would like to thank the team at Melbourne University Publishing: Nathan Hollier, CEO, Cathryn Smith, senior editor, Duncan Fardon, publishing assistant, Meaghan Amor, copy editor, Paige Amor, proofreader, and Daniel New, designer, for their vision, commitment and hard work.

We dedicate this book to the memory of our mothers: Patricia Carter and Pauline Oswald-Jacobs.

An undated still life by Burke, revealing her continued exploration of colour and mark making.

Authors

NANETTE CARTER

Nanette Carter completed a master's degree in art history, focusing on the development of modern design in Melbourne in the 1930s. She subsequently researched and wrote on postwar interiors by designer and artist Clement Meadmore. Her 2015 PhD on the emergence of DIY culture in the postwar period in Australia was jointly supervised by the School of Historical Studies and the Faculty of Architecture, Building and Planning at the University of Melbourne. In addition to researching and writing about Australia's design history, Nanette has curated exhibitions for Swinburne University of Technology—'Pen to Pixel'—and for Heide Museum of Modern Art—'Savage Luxury: Modernist Design in Melbourne 1930–1939'. Nanette is an adjunct scholar connected to the School of Design, Swinburne University.

ROBYN OSWALD-JACOBS

Independent scholar Robyn Oswald-Jacobs completed a diploma in textile design at RMIT before undertaking a research master's degree on textile designer Frances Burke. In part as a result of this research the Textile Resource Collection: Australian Fashion and Textile Design was established by the Department of Fashion and Textile Design at RMIT. Managed by Robyn, the centre collected, exhibited and published archival material, later forming the foundation of the RMIT Design Archives. Robyn also designed and delivered cultural heritage projects for RMIT, including re-opening the RMIT Capitol Theatre in 1999 and the development of the RMIT/National Trust Heritage Legal Precinct, Russell Street, Melbourne. Robyn was subsequently appointed business development director (new business) for FutureBrand Australia.

Index

THE MIEGUNYAH PRESS

This book was designed by Daniel New
The text was typeset by Daniel New
The text was set in 11 point Minion Pro
with 13.4 points of leading
The text is printed on 128 gsm Matt Art
This book was edited by Meaghan Amor

THE
MIEGUNYAH
PRESS